R. W. Beers

The Mormon puzzle, and how to solve it

R. W. Beers

The Mormon puzzle, and how to solve it

ISBN/EAN: 9783743338395

Manufactured in Europe, USA, Canada, Australia, Japa

Cover: Foto ©Lupo / pixelio.de

Manufactured and distributed by brebook publishing software (www.brebook.com)

R. W. Beers

The Mormon puzzle, and how to solve it

THE

MORMON PUZZLE;

AND HOW TO SOLVE IT.

BY

REV. R. W. BEERS, A.M.,

PASTOR OF THE PRESBYTERIAN CHURCH, ELKTON, MD.

"A disposition to preserve, and an ability to improve, taken together, would be my standard of a statesman."—EDMUND BURKE.

FUNK & WAGNALLS, Publishers.

CHICAGO :   NEW YORK :   LONDON :
TIMES BUILDING.   18 & 20 ASTOR PLACE.   44 FLEET STREET.

1887

Entered, according to Act of Congre'
By FUNK & WAGN
In the Office of the Librarian of Cong?

To My Parents,

TO WHOSE SELF-SACRIFICE AND DEVOTION I OWE SO MUCH,
THIS VOLUME IS LOVINGLY

Dedicated.

PREFACE.

The following pages have at least the merit of being addressed to a subject of living interest to the American people. Perhaps with the single exception of the labor problem, the Mormon problem is the most important question before the people of our country at the present time. It is a problem which has thus far been unsolvable by the moralist, the statesman, and the politician. It still remains a Puzzle. No feasible plan has yet been hit upon for getting rid of it.

From the past failures to solve it, it would seem that the problem has either not been studied from the proper standpoint, or has been misunderstood. Accordingly, we instituted a careful study of the problem in all its different phases, and endeavored to conduct our investigation in a fair and impartial manner. In doing so we consulted the leading authorities, both Mormon and non-Mormon, and must here acknowledge our indebtedness especially to "New Light on Mormonism," by Mrs. Ellen E. Dickinson; "Illiteracy and Mormonism," by Henry Randall Waite; Professor Coyner's "Handbook on Mormonism;" Schaff-Herzog's "Encyclopædia of Religious Knowledge;" and back files of the *Independent*, *Christian Union*, and *Deseret News*—all of which were freely used in the preparation of this volume.

It has the merit of being the product of about two years' careful thought and research. Most of the writings on Mormonism at the present day are the result of a few days' study of the subject on the field of Utah;

but, apart from the insufficient time which such authors devote to the study of so knotty a problem, their minds are very apt to be warped by the people among whom their lot is cast during their short visit there, and they almost inevitably present a one-sided view of the question.

Thus, some have fallen into the hands of *the Mormons;* and they have returned from Utah delighted, and let fall from their lips naught but encomiums for the priesthood and apologies for the Mormon system. Many of our legislators have in this way been the dupes of the Mormon priesthood. On this subject the much-lamented *Mary Clemmer* wrote the following pungent lines:

"Legislators constantly passing to and from California find Salt Lake City a most attractive stopping-place. The Mormon hierarchy, sly, cunning, astute, to the last limit of human nature, is ever sharply on the lookout for these potent summer visitors. 'Prophets' and 'apostles' board every train of cars that enters Utah bearing an important traveller. The freedom of the city, the hospitality of the show 'happy families,' who are never taken by surprise on an off-day of misery, is lavished upon the ingenuous guest. . . . The facts impressed upon his senses, as well as his understanding, are those of great industry, thrift, wealth, prosperity—of shrewd men and of seemingly happy women. Indeed, their supreme occupation while with him is to prove to him that they *are* happy, while the men are equally busy in spreading before him the vast resources of both the Church and the Territory. This man, who is one of many men whose voice and vote tells upon human affairs, leaves the Territory at last deeply in debt personally for favors received and mentally somewhat dazed by the material profitableness of a religious system that he wishes to denounce, but does not pretend to understand."

On the other hand, many have fallen into the hands of *bitter non-Mormons* during their brief stay in Utah; and their minds have been filled with horrible stories of the brutalities and crimes of the Mormon people. They have returned disgusted, and have uttered harsh tirades against the whole Mormon system and all who believe in it, declaring that it should be utterly exterminated, even by the sword. Of their utterances and writings the official organ of the Mormon Church, the *Deseret News*, in its issue of July 21st, 1886, reasonably complains. It says : " Salt Lake City is not Utah, and conversation with a little knot of anti-Mormons does not impart much accurate information on ' Mormonism.' The books that are written by tourists who come in by the cars, take a hack, a ride around town, a sniff at the lake, a glance at the Temple, and a guess at the situation, and who make up their data from other publications and the yarns of persons who take delight in filling up travellers with blood-curdling Munchausenisms, are not likely to correct the public mind on a subject about which there is more misinformation than almost any other. . . . And these books are not any less reliable than the remarks and tales and remedies that fall from the lips of men who spend a few weeks in a given locality in one Utah town, and then go to the world and air their great experience and knowledge about the ' Mormons ' through ' a protracted residence in Utah.' "

It was our desire to avoid both Scylla and Charybdis —to treat the subject with an unbiased mind—to get the real facts, and then propound, if possible, a solution to the problem. We have not been in actual contact either with Mormons or non-Mormons. We have not been on the field of Utah at all, and believe that the value of this volume as an impartial study is thereby greatly enhanced. Furthermore, while we have avoided the narrow views of the subject which would almost inevitably have resulted from a personal visit to Utah, we have been in communication both with leading Mormons and non-Mormons on the field, and have in that way acquired all the *reliable* information which could have been obtained by a *long residence* there.

The result of our long and careful study, which was prosecuted while we were engaged in regular pastoral duties, was first given to the members of our own congregation in a series of lectures on week-day evenings ; and while they have since then been enlarged and carefully revised, they still have the free oratorical style which, though inexcusable in a work prepared exclusively for publication, may be pardoned in an oral lecture.

The solution of the "*Mormon Puzzle*" to which we have arrived is given forth with the firm conviction that it is practicable, and if carried out in its various parts would peaceably overcome all the bad qualities belonging to Mormonism, which are the sole cause of the puzzle now before the people of our country. Nevertheless, we do not anticipate for our views the indorsement of the extremists on either side ; but we believe they will commend themselves to the fair-minded people of our land ; at least, it is hoped that all minds open to conviction may find something in these pages worthy of their serious thought. We only ask that the reader may adopt the precept of Bacon : "Read not to contradict and confute ; nor to believe and take for granted ; but to weigh and consider."

THE AUTHOR.

PRESBYTERIAN PARSONAGE, ELKTON, MD.

TABLE OF CONTENTS.

INTRODUCTORY REMARKS.

PART I.

HISTORY OF MORMONISM.

CHAPTER I.
PAGE

Alleged Origin of Mormonism—Joseph Smith's Early Life—Finding the Peek-stone—Visited by an Angel—Received the Golden Plates—Was Smith a Swindler or an Enthusiast?—"Book of Mormon" Published, and Mormon Church Established—Smith's First Alleged Miracle—Rigdon Joins the Mormons—Mormonism Compared to Mohammedanism............ 25

CHAPTER II.
HISTORY OF MORMONISM (*continued*).

The First Hegira from Palmyra to Kirtland—The First Temple—Rapid Growth of the Mormon Church—Brigham Young and other Missionaries Sent to Foreign Lands—The Name "Latter-day Saints" Adopted—Smith and Rigdon Compelled to Flee from Kirtland—*The Second Hegira*—The "Danites" Organized—Rapid Increase of the Mormons in Missouri—Jealousy of the Missourians—Mormons Driven across the Missouri River by a Mob—Their Property Confiscated—Their Leaders Imprisoned... 38

CHAPTER III.
HISTORY OF MORMONISM (*continued*).

The Third Hegira—Sufferings of the Mormons during their Journey into Illinois—An Account of the Murder of Mormons

—Influence of this Persecution on the Minds of Mormons at the Present Time—*Nauvoo*—Its Location—Its Growth—The Second Mormon Temple Begun—Other Public Buildings—Laziness Whittled out of Nauvoo—Internal Dissensions Among the Mormons—Political Troubles—Smith Nominated for President of the United States—Warrants Issued against the Mormon Leaders—Constable Driven out of Nauvoo—Civil War Threatened—Smith Asked to Submit to Trial—Murder of Joseph Smith and his Brother—Rigdon Excommunicated, and Brigham Young Made Leader—Consecration of the "Pride of the Valley".................. 45

CHAPTER IV.
HISTORY OF MORMONISM (*concluded*).

The Fourth Hegira—Young's Shrewd Plan of a Western Kingdom—Nauvoo's Sad End—Journey of the Mormons to Council Bluffs—Young's Forethought—The Trip of the Pioneers Across the Wilderness—The Halt at Salt Lake Valley—Young Leads the Remaining Mormons from Council Bluffs to Salt Lake—Their Entertainment during their March—Folly of the Illinoisans in Driving them out into the Wilderness—Probable Result of Tolerance of the Mormons—Character of the Mormons—Life Begun Anew in Salt Lake Valley—Salt Lake City Established—Mills and Workshops Established and the Great Temple Begun—Increase of the Mormon Population—Value of their Property in Utah—Public Schools—A Final Brief Glance at their History—How the Mormon Puzzle will not be Solved.. 54

PART II.

THE POLITICAL PUZZLE.

CHAPTER V.

Mormonism a Theocracy—Manœuvring for Office the Cause of the Expulsion of the Mormons from Missouri and Nauvoo—The "State of Deseret" Formed—Lands Illegally Obtained—Brigham's Movable House—Government Officials Compelled to

Flee—Federal Troops Sent—The Oath of Disloyalty—The Endowment Rites—The American Flag at Half-mast—The Control of the Nation their Aim—The Political Puzzle Stated—Its Causes—Necessity of Government Action... 67

CHAPTER VI.

THE POLITICAL PUZZLE (*continued*).

The Possible Remedies—The Military Remedy—The Government Responsible for the Situation in Utah—The Disfranchisement of Polygamists—Federal Trustees for the Mormon Church Corporation—Confiscation of Unlawful Funds—False Statements About Mormons—Letters from the Two Bancrofts—The Dissolution of the Emigrating Fund Company—The Federal Commission Remedy—The Woodburn Bill, or Idaho Statute.. 77

CHAPTER VII.

THE POLITICAL PUZZLE (*concluded*).

Objections to Proposed Remedies—*Gladstone* on "Coercion"—A NEW PLAN ADVOCATED—*The Abolition of Female Suffrage*—*A National Colonization Scheme*—Natural Resources of Utah—Superiority of the Colonization Plan over Others—*The Establishment of National Free Schools*—Ignorance the Keystone of Mormon Despotism—Public Schools in Utah used for Mormon Purposes—Proposed Federal Superintendent of Schools in Utah—Territorial Schools Too Few—Necessity of Government Action—Prejudice Disarmed by this Plan—THE POLITICAL PUZZLE SOLVED... 91

PART III.

THE SOCIAL PUZZLE.

CHAPTER VIII.

Polygamy only one of the Mormon Social Evils—Their Social System *a System of Bondage*—Contrary to Natural Law—Contrary to the Spirit of the Age—PERSONAL BONDAGE of the Mormons—Missionaries *Must* Go on Duty—Dictation of the

Priesthood with Regard to Boarders and Rents—Immigrants Under their Control—All Members Subject to Church Orders—Power of the Church over Daily Business—Mormon Mining Contractors—MENTAL BONDAGE of the Mormons—Converts Illiterate—The Mormon Church the Opponent of Free Education—No Independent Thought—Excommunication of Henry Lawrence and Others.................................... 107

CHAPTER IX.
THE SOCIAL PUZZLE (continued).

MORAL BONDAGE of the Mormons—Implicit Obedience to the Priesthood Enjoined—*Crimes Committed* at their Command—Murders—The Mountain Meadows Massacre—Lee's Confession—A Mormon Carpenter's Confession—Theft—Falsehood—Perjury—Why was Polygamy Promulgated?—Why is Polygamy Practised?... 118

CHAPTER X.
THE SOCIAL PUZZLE (continued).

Reasons why Mormon Slavery is Maintained—Hope of Earthly Gain—Complete Organization of the Mormon Church—Prospect of Promotion in Office as a Bribe—Fear of Earthly Loss—System of Espionage—Apostasy Formerly Punished by Death—Mode of Inflicting the Punishment—Social Ostracism—Religious Conviction the Mainstay of the Mormon Social System. 131

CHAPTER XI.
THE SOCIAL PUZZLE (concluded).

THE SOLUTION OF THE SOCIAL PUZZLE—Mormon Slavery and Negro Slavery Compared—The Duty of the Government to Break up Mormon Slavery—The Remedy the Same as for the Political Evils of Mormonism—Brigham Young Opposed to Immigration of Gentiles—A Growing Spirit of Restlessness—Necessity of Surrounding the Youth with an Atmosphere of Freedom—*Personal Bondage* of the Mormons Overcome by Gentile Colonization—Social Ostracism no Longer Dreaded—*Mental Bondage* Overcome by National Schools and Colonization—*Moral Bondage* Overcome by the Same Means—This Policy not to be Confounded with the Let-Alone Policy—An

Apparent Policy of Toleration—The Alarmist's Cry and its Answer—The Mormon Standpoint not to be Overlooked—The Cry of Unconstitutionality—The Proposed Polygamy Amendment to the Constitution—The Cry of Religious Persecution—Imprisonment Preferred to Sacrifice of Principle—Law Impotent to Break up Polygamy—Supposed Captivity of Mormon Women a Mistake—Mass-Meeting of Mormon Women to Plead for Polygamy—*Senator Hoar* on the Solution of the Social Puzzle—How the Law Should be Enforced and its Probable Effect—Superiority of the Colonization Plan over any Other Plan—Its Effectiveness Proved by the Oneida Community—*The Social Puzzle Solved*—The Duty of the Nation, the Citizen, and the Church.. 138

PART IV.

THE RELIGIOUS PUZZLE.

CHAPTER XII.

The Religious Aspects of Mormonism Paramount—General Ignorance Concerning the Mormon Religious System — SOURCES OF THEIR DOCTRINES—Revelation, not Reason, the Primary Source—All Religions Founded on Revelation—Sacred Books—The Mormon Bible—The "Book of Mormon"—Migrations of Jews to America—Visit of Jesus to America —"Book of Doctrine and Covenants"—The "Living Oracles"............... 161

CHAPTER XIII.

THE RELIGIOUS PUZZLE (*continued*).

MORMON DOCTRINES—Their Idea of God—Plurality of Gods—Mormon Sunday-School Hymn Concerning Smith—The Preexistence of Souls—The Doctrine of Polygamy—Practised on the Plea of Self-Sacrifice and Ambition—Necessity of Preaching their Gospel to All—Preaching to the Dead—Baptismal Regeneration—Baptism for the Dead—Mormon Priesthood Necessary to Salvation—Melchizedek and Aaronic Priesthood—Mormon Endowments—Blood Atonement—Doctrine of "The Fulness of Times".. 168

CHAPTER XIV.

THE RELIGIOUS PUZZLE (*continued*).

Professor Coyner's Analysis of Mormonism—Rev. Dr. McNiece's Analysis—Reasons for the Growth and Tenacity of Mormonism—The Christian Element its Chief Source of Strength—No Mormon Converts from Heathenism—Protestantism the Source of its Recruits—Bible Doctrines in the Mormon "Catechism for Children"—The Mormon Articles of Faith—The Mormon Heresy Compared to Gnosticism in the Early Christian Church—A Clue to the Solution of the Religious Puzzle.............. 181

CHAPTER XV.

THE RELIGIOUS PUZZLE (*concluded*).

The Character of Efforts Hitherto put Forth to Solve the Puzzle—What has been Accomplished—The Plan Somewhere Defective—Mormonism to be Reformed, not Destroyed—Why Mormons will not Listen to Christian Missionaries—Moody and Sankey's Meetings in Salt Lake City—*The Deseret Evening News* on Bishop Tuttle's Sermon—Mormonism a Perversion of Christianity—The Educational and Colonization Scheme best Fitted to Reform it—Proved by Comparing Roman Catholicism in the United States with Roman Catholicism in Mexico or Brazil—The Probable Effect of a Larger Intelligence—The Probable Effect of the Introduction of Gentile Colonies—The Religious Puzzle Solved—The Duty of the Hour............ 188

INTRODUCTORY REMARKS.

"SEARCH for the truth is the noblest occupation of man."—MADAME DE STAËL.

"NEVER suppose yourself to understand the ignorance of another so long as you are ignorant of his understanding."—COLERIDGE.

INTRODUCTORY REMARKS.

He was a sage and a seer who remarked concerning Mormonism : "It presents a problem which the wisest politician has failed to solve, and whose outcome lies in the mystery of the future." It is acknowledged to be the Great Modern Abomination, the most pernicious heresy of this century ; and yet in ten years from its origin its devotees numbered thousands, and Joseph Smith, its founder, predicted that it was to be the religious faith of the Western Continent. To-day its membership numbers its hundreds of thousands, its organizations extend over a large part of the globe, and the most careless observer of the times must realize that this institution has become one of the gravest and most difficult religious, social, and political puzzles of the day.

Throughout our whole land it is universally despised and execrated ; and if popular odium could extinguish it, it would speedily be sunk in the slimy depths of the Great Salt Lake. But thus far it has successfully withstood even the fiercest opposition. That Mormonism is not the weak, empty, insignificant thing which it is so generally assumed to be must be obvious to any one who sets himself seriously to account for its origin, its growth, and its present position and influence. There *must* be more in the system than is popularly supposed ; otherwise the organization could never have grown to be what it is, nor could it now stand up so persistently and even prosperously in the presence of such universal opposition.

Very much of what is said and written concerning Mormonism amounts to but very little because of its obvious failure to understand what it denounces; and it will be well for us at the outset to notice A FEW OF THE MISTAKES CONCERNING MORMONISM that are now current.

1. Most people talk as if *Mormonism and polygamy are synonymous*, whereas polygamy is only a comparatively trifling and non-essential part of Mormonism. For ten years after the Church was founded, it was not heard of; and it was not openly taught for twenty years. If it could be brought to a sudden conclusion either by a new revelation, or stamped out by law, Mormonism, with its preposterous claims, its absorption of things political in things ecclesiastical, its ideas, some of them more than heathenish, its intensely secular spirit, its standard of morality lamentably low—MORMONISM, in its worst phases, and in what it is most damaging to souls and fullest of peril to the Republic, would still stand unscathed.

2. And then, in strict accordance with that false notion, is the idea that *the Mormons are a mere horde of sensualized barbarians*, and should consequently be dealt with in the most severe manner imaginable; whereas, the fact is that the great mass of Mormons do not practise polygamy, and *never have done so*. It is true that, as a people, they are chargeable with the gravest crimes; and yet they have been perpetrated by *the few*, while *the many* have been, and are, devoted to what *they believe* to be the true and the right. Contrasts are often drawn (and truthfully drawn, too) by their preachers between "the unworldly lives of the Saints and the evil practices of the Gentiles," and pertinent examples are given of aberration from rectitude of men intrusted with the making of our laws or those who minister at the altars of

divine worship, until they regard themselves as clothed with the resplendent robes of righteousness. Perhaps the worst thing that can be said of the mass of the Mormons is that they are poor, ignorant, and superstitious, and therefore an easy prey to a corrupt and infamous priesthood. But many who are equally poor, ignorant, and superstitious can be found in every State in the Union, and in some States they are far greater in number than in Utah.

3. Then, too, there is another mistaken idea concerning Mormonism. The assertion is often made that *it is an exotic—an importation from the Old World*, and especially that the pollutions of polygamy may justly be charged to the English, Swedes, and Danes. But this is not true. Facts compel a conclusion far less flattering. Smith and his system are essentially a New World product. It took its rise in a region lying between the birthplace of the Rochester Rappings, from which Modern Spiritualism sprang, and the seat of the Oneida Community. It had much in common, too, with the great Campbellite movement, which antedated it only by five or ten years, and from which it received a large number of important accessions. Millerism and Shakerism were also near relatives and neighbors. Yea, more—in Mormonism we have an obnoxious plant which *sprang from Puritan seed*, though it first *took root* in the Empire State. Joseph Smith, its founder, and Brigham Young, its greatest leader, were both born in Vermont. At least ninety per cent of the converts gathered during the first ten years (1830-40) were of New England descent. In 1860, out of a population in Utah of some 70,000, it is affirmed that 10,000 were born in New York and 20,000 in New England; while in the legislature, of thirty-six members, thirteen were

born in New York, six in Massachusetts, and five in Vermont. And in an editorial written less than two years ago, the official Mormon Church paper states that "of twenty-eight men constituting the general authorities of the Church, twenty-four were born in the United States and eighteen were of New England birth or origin. Of twenty-seven 'Stakes of Zion,' twenty have presidents born under the Stars and Stripes, and a large majority are of New England parentage. The founders were mostly descendants of the Pilgrim Fathers; the leading minds are nearly all of Puritan blood." It is, however, some comfort to know that, since polygamy was accepted and proclaimed, recruiting from among the sons of the Pilgrims has almost altogether ceased; and yet it is well for those of us who are so boastful of what Puritan thought and energy have accomplished for America to remember that this greatest abomination of our land is also a product of the thought and energy of the descendants of the Pilgrims—an institution, therefore, ESSENTIALLY AMERICAN.

4. It is also commonly supposed at the present day that *about nine tenths of the Mormons are foreign rather than American;* but the last census gives Utah a foreign-born population of 43,933 and a native-born population of 99,974. Making allowance for the probable preponderance of the native element among the Gentile population, and allowing a large subtraction from the latter figure on account of the thousands of children born of foreign parentage in Utah, it would still be probable that the native is, at least, equal to the foreign fraction in the general aggregate. And this will be the more readily admitted when it is remembered that, while public attention has been more attracted toward the recent importations of converts from Europe,

the earlier Mormons in Utah were almost exclusively American. So far as personal prominence goes, if not in numbers, *the native element has always been, and is now, entirely predominant.*

Since, then, there are so many common mistakes with reference to Mormonism, let us endeavor to look at the system fully in a fair and impartial manner, considering *its marvellous history*, in the first place ; and, then, *its threefold character* as a religious, social, and political system, with which we have to deal not only as patriots, but also as Christians.

PART I.

HISTORY OF MORMONISM.

"Examine history, for it is 'Philosophy teaching by experience.'"
—Carlyle.

"'Tis strange, but true; for truth is always strange,
    Stranger than fiction."   Byron.

CHAPTER I.

Alleged origin of Mormonism—Joseph Smith's early life—Finding the peek-stone—Visited by an angel—Received the golden plates—Was Smith a swindler or an enthusiast?—"Book of Mormon" published, and Mormon Church established—Smith's first alleged miracle—Rigdon joins the Mormons—Mormonism compared to Mohammedanism.

IT is acknowledged by all who have given careful thought to the subject, that Mormonism presents us with a very extraordinary civilization and the most peculiar religion under the sun; but *its history* is as unique and peculiar as the system itself, and is well worthy the attention of the philosopher as well as the student of human nature and human history.

Its alleged origin was miraculous, and calculated to inspire its followers with wonder, admiration, and awe. As Moses, the founder of Judaism, received the two tables of the moral law, which constituted the brief Bible of the Israelites, from the hand of God Himself, while the lightning blazed around his head and the earth quaked beneath his feet, so Joseph Smith (it is alleged) received his Golden Bible from the hand of an angel on the Hill Cummorah near Palmyra, N. Y., amid thunder and lightning. He is represented in an old picture as kneeling on the steep incline of that hill, the wind blowing his long hair out in all directions, and his eyes big with surprise. Above him in a cloud is the placid angel, gazing intently upon the future prophet, who is eagerly taking his credentials from a cemented stone chest which had been buried some 1400 years, while out of the overshadowing cloud have come forth zigzags of lightning which are playing around both Joseph and the angel.

The name of the angel was Moroni, and he informed Smith that the fate of the early inhabitants of America was written on golden tablets within that chest, and that these could be read only by the aid of some wonderful stone spectacles called "Urim and Thummim," which were also in the chest. Smith said that on opening the precious box he found six golden tablets eighteen inches square held together by rings at the back, and also the stone spectacles to decipher the tablets; and besides these, the sword of Laban and a "breastplate" which had been brought from Jerusalem by the early inhabitants of our land were inclosed in the chest.

The hill on which these sacred things were found is at present known as Gold Bible Hill, and the true Mormon venerates it as a sacred spot, and travels from afar to see its quiet but not remarkable beauty. It is a conical elevation several hundred feet in height, and in its isolation and peculiar form bears a certain resemblance to an extinct volcano. It is smooth and green to the very top, from which there is a picturesque view of hills and dales in all directions. It is situated in Wayne County, N. Y., four miles from the village of Palmyra and three miles from the home of the false prophet who has given it its present fame.

Like all other prophets, whether true or false, Joseph Smith was of very humble origin. His father was a cooper by trade, and he dug wells and worked on the neighboring farms when he could. His mother washed by the day, but it is said that her employers were careful to have the clothes in before dark, as experience had taught them they would disappear if left on the lines over night. The whole family made baskets and maple sugar, and raised and sold garden vegetables.

The youthful Joseph assisted generally, and (it is alleged) was an adept in robbing hen-roosts and orchards. It seems that when quite young he could read, but not write. His two standard volumes were "The Life of Stephen Burroughs," the clerical scoundrel, and the autobiography of Captain Kidd, the pirate. The latter work was eagerly and often perused. At an early age he committed the following lines to memory, which seemed to give him great pleasure:

> "My name was Robert Kidd,
> As I sailed, as I sailed;
> And most wickedly I did,
> And God's laws I did forbid,
> As I sailed, as I sailed."

A certain superstitious feeling concerning the Smith family existed in the minds of their more ignorant neighbors on account of the reputation which Mrs. Smith had for telling fortunes. She seems to have been a woman full of odd conceits and superstitions, while at the same time she possessed a great deal of natural talent; and Joseph resembled his mother in mental quickness and imaginative power.

When he was scarcely fifteen years old, while he was watching the digging of a well, he said that he found a peculiarly shaped stone that resembled a child's foot in its outlines. It must have resembled the stone foot of Buddha at Bangkok, Siam. At any rate, it has well been said that this foot "has left footprints on the sands of time." This little stone, afterward known as the "peek-stone" and the "Palmyra seer-stone," has been called "the acorn of the Mormon oak."

For some time Joseph Smith obtained a subsistence

by means of that stone. In a kneeling posture, with a bandage over his eyes (so luminous was the sight without it), with the stone in a large, white stove-pipe hat, and this hat in front of his face, he claimed to see very remarkable sights, such as buried treasures of gold and silver. He could trace stolen property, tell where herds of cattle had strayed and where water could be found. With the "peeker" he carried a rod of witch-hazel, which assisted him in the discovery of water.

This state of affairs continued for some time. Then he disappeared, and for four years his life is involved in much mystery; but during that time he is known to have been in both Onondaga and Shenango counties, N. Y., since his name appears in the criminal records of both as a vagabond. While he was wandering through the country during those years of mystery, he doubtless heard the theories (as they were a common topic of conversation at the time) that were afloat to account for the peopling of America—the traditions collected from the Indians, the Hebrew traditions among them, the discovery of ruined cities and temples in Central America, the relics of pottery, and the bricks and stumps of axe-cut trees buried far beneath the surface of the Mississippi.

During that time, also, he became interested in the great revivals that prevailed in the churches of the different denominations in the vicinity of his home at Palmyra. In 1821 five of the Smith family were awakened, and united with the Presbyterian Church. Joseph, in his own account of his early life, says that he "became somewhat partial to the Methodist sect," but he was not able to decide which was right. In his bewilderment he gave himself up to prayer for days, that the truth might be made known to him among all the conflicting opinions that he heard among these different sects; and finally a heavenly messenger bade him not to join any sect. And three years afterward, on September 22d, 1823, another celestial visitant outlined to him about the golden plates he was to find and the prophet he was to be. He was told that the North American Indians were a remnant of Israel, the descendants of a certain family of Jews that emigrated from Jerusalem in the time of Zedekiah, and were miraculously led across the Eastern Ocean ; and he was also told that before they had fallen off from the faith a priest and prophet named Mormon had, by direction of God, drawn up an abstract of their national records and religious opinions, and buried it, and that he himself was selected to recover and publish it to the world. He was also told that it contained many prophecies relating to these "latter days," and would give instructions as to "the gathering of the Saints" into a temporal and spiritual kingdom, preparatory to the second coming of the Messiah, which was *at hand.*

From that time on he declares that his days and nights were filled with "visions," "voices," and "angels;" and, following the direction of an angel, on the night of September 22d, 1827, amid a grand display of celestial pyrotechnics, he received from the hand of the angel Moroni, the son of Mormon, a chest that contained a number of golden tablets with inscriptions, and with them a pair of stone spectacles by means of which he was to decipher the characters. It is asserted that these plates were seen by eleven persons, but all of them except three were members of Smith's family or his near neighbors. The plates themselves disappeared soon after the publication of the "Book of Mormon," and it is understood that the angel took them again into his custody.

The tablets, Smith said, were covered with hieroglyphics, which he called the "reformed Egyptian" language. A document was actually exhibited as a confirmation of this assertion, and was seen by Professor Charles Anthon, of Columbia College, New York City, who in a letter dated February 17th, 1834, relates that it was in fact a singular scroll, containing a mixture of Greek, Hebrew, and Roman letters, with crosses and flourishes, and a Mexican calendar given by Humboldt, but altered so that it could not be well recognized.

For more than two years, by the aid of the stone spectacles, Smith was engaged in translating the hieroglyphics into English. In March, 1830, the translation was given into the printer's hands, was published under the title of the "Book of Mormon," and that book is the corner-stone of that great MODERN DELUSION called MORMONISM. A *delusion* the writer prefers to call it rather than "*the Latter-day swindle*," as Joseph Cook and many others denominate it.

There are TWO VIEWS that may be taken of Joseph Smith by the Christian world. One is that he was *a base swindler*, and concocted the Mormon scheme with the express purpose of deluding the people; the other is that he was *a religious enthusiast*, deceived and deluded himself. Arguments may be adduced in support of either theory, and which are the stronger is a question which every man must settle for himself.

1. On the one hand, it may be said that Smith's former life is in strict accord with the theory that his scheme was a deliberate fraud; for he swindled many of his neighbors with his "peek-stone."

But, on the other hand, it may be said that it is not so certain that he was not himself deceived with regard to that matter also. At any rate, his naturally superstitious and imaginative mind, which he inherited from his mother, would strongly favor the idea that he really thought he saw visions and heard voices. Even Joseph Cook says, in an address delivered in Salt Lake City, May 17th, 1884 : ." I am not sure that he did not have in his experience some spiritistic manifestations, which he mistook for a revelation ; but I am sure that if he had any superhuman revelation, it came from below the earth rather than from above it."

2. Again, in support of the swindling theory, it may be said that, apart from the "peek-stone" business, his previous immoral life and ignorance favors the idea that he was a base villain ; but, on the other hand, it might be said that that is only another form of the old mistaken notion that "no good thing can come out of Nazareth."

3. Then, too, it might be said that Mormonism was regarded as a swindle by the people generally who lived right around him and were acquainted with him and his character ; but, on the other hand, it may be said that that is no proof whatever that the Mormon scheme *was a fraud*, but only another evidence of the truth of the well-known proverb : " A prophet is not without honor except in his own country."

4. Again, it may be said that Joseph Smith was evidently a swindler, because most of the "Book of Mormon" was copied from the manuscript of one Solomon Spaulding, a Presbyterian clergyman of Western Pennsylvania. Between 1809 and 1813 he lived in Northeastern Ohio, and, being fond of the study of archæology, he became intensely interested in the ancient mounds and fortifications which abound in that region, and he himself opened up one near his own dwelling. Since these mounds gave unmistakable evidences of the exist-

ence of an extinct race higher in the scale of civilization than the present American Indians, he adopted the theory that this Continent was peopled by a colony of ancient Israelites, and in a time of infirm health he wrote an historical romance embodying that theory.

The style of the book was a clumsy imitation of our English Bible, and the book originally bore the title of "THE MANUSCRIPT FOUND," the idea at the root of the book being that Mr. Spaulding discovered among other prehistoric mementoes in one of the earth-mounds near his house an ancient manuscript which gave an account of the wanderings and sufferings of the Israelites after coming to America, and he merely translated the story as contained in *the manuscript that was found*. He tried to have it published and took it to a printing-office in Pittsburg, where it remained for some time. It is said that in his book there was much repetition of phrases common in Scripture, such as, "And it came to pass," and also that he used the names Lehi, Nephi, Moroni, Lamanites, etc., which names are all found in the "Book of Mormon."

It is supposed that this manuscript in some way unknown fell into the hands of Smith, and that he and his confederates introduced into it the religious part of the "Book of Mormon" touching the establishment of another church.

But, on the other hand, it may be said that that has ever been strenuously denied by the Mormons, and *has never yet been proved*. The editor of the *Independent* says, in the issue of January 7th, 1886, that Mrs. Spaulding herself was in total ignorance concerning the fate of "The Manuscript Found." During the year 1834, when the events must have been comparatively well fixed in her memory, "she *thinks* it was once taken to the printing-office of Patterson & Lambdin [in Pittsburg]; but whether it was ever brought back to the house again she is quite uncertain." The fact is, that from the time it went into the hands of the printer its history is lost. It is true that it *might* have fallen into the hands of Smith or his confederates, but it is just as likely that it did not. All that we have learned of its contents has been obtained from the memory of persons who had read it or heard it read fifty or more years ago, none of whom are now living. The manuscript itself is not known to have been seen since it was given to the printer. Whether it was destroyed, or is still in existence, no one knows positively.

The only manuscript of Solomon Spaulding's yet found is the one recently discovered in Honolulu, Sandwich Islands; but concerning this, Rev. Sereno E. Bishop, of Honolulu, says: "Unlike the ' Book of Mormon,' the Spaulding manuscript is not sham Hebraistic, but in ordinary English. It contains perhaps no quotations from the Bible, unlike the other, which transfers large portions of Isaiah and other books. Both devise a number of uncouth names for their characters; both record a series of desperate wars; both narrate a voyage across the Atlantic in ancient times and a settlement in North America." Evidently the "Book of Mormon" was not copied from *that manuscript*, and the Mormons welcomed it as disproving the Spaulding origin of their sacred book, and have had an edition of it published.

5. Those who believe in the swindling theory will only say that *Spaulding had more than one manuscript*, and the one recently found is not the one that the "Book of Mormon" was taken from. Besides, the similarity of names and the account of the wars mentioned in this

manuscript and the "Book of Mormon" would go far to substantiate the idea that *the " Book of Mormon" was copied from some manuscript of Spaulding's.*

But, again, it may be said that there is no doubt that Joseph Smith was at one time in the employ of the brother of Mrs. Spaulding, at whose house she was then residing, just after her husband's death. Of course he heard all the talk of the house, and much was said concerning the romance by Solomon Spaulding, which all regarded as wonderful both in style and substance. This talk would naturally make a great impression upon the superstitious mind of Smith. He would be very apt to take it as absolute truth, and *without seeing the manuscript at all,* was prepared to use what he knew of it in getting up one of the greatest delusions in the history of modern times.

6. Moreover, there can be no question at all concerning the fact that his mind was strangely exercised by the popular religious movement that swept through the country at that time, and his imaginative and superstitious mind was deeply impressed by the eloquence of the different evangelists. He became familiar with biblical language, and followed the inclination of those about him to listen to any new-fangled doctrine; and surely the religious teachings of the "Book of Mormon" are positive evidence of the strongest character that the mind of Smith and his coadjutors were greatly influenced by the doctrinal questions that were being agitated at that time in Central New York—Calvinism, Universalism, Methodism, Millerism, Romanism, Campbellism, and other *isms.*

Millerism in particular was attracting great attention at that time, and so they incorporated into the "Book of Mormon" its leading tenets—viz.: that the millennium was close at hand; that the Indians were to be converted; and that America was to be the final gathering-place of the Saints, who were to assemble at the New Jerusalem, somewhere in the interior of the Continent.

Perhaps, in the absence of positive proof to the contrary, it is the part of Christian charity to regard the founder of Mormonism as a strange fanatic and *religious enthusiast of the same general type as Mohammed.*

But however that may be, the publication of the " Book of Mormon" created an intense excitement in Central and Western New York; for the public mind was at that time prepared for any new religious sensation.'

Soon after the book appeared the Mormon Church was formally organized at the house of one Peter Whitmer in Fayette, Seneca County, N. Y. The membership consisted of only six, all men—the prophet and two of his brothers, two Whitmers, and Oliver Cowdery, a school-teacher of that neighborhood. They said it was 1800 years to a day since the resurrection of Christ, and they professed to believe that their church was the " Church of Christ" once more restored to the earth, holding the keys of authority, and having the power to bind and loose and seal on earth and in heaven.

Within a week or two Smith added to his reputation by performing the first great miracle of the " new dispensation," which was performed on a man whose visage and limbs were frightfully distorted by a demoniacal possession. Smith commanded the evil spirits to leave him in the name of Christ, and the man said : " I see them going right through the roof." This established the fact in the minds of certain people that Smith really had a divine mission; but at the First Mormon Conference in June, Smith found himself at the head of a visible church of only thirty members. This small number of adherents showed that converts were not to be rapidly made in that vicinity. Still, the excitement concerning the new Mormon doctrines spread through Western New York into Northern and Eastern Ohio. Members were sent West to preach and found churches wherever people would listen to them, and they made many converts.

In December, 1830, Sidney Rigdon, a Campbellite preacher near Mentor, O., became a convert. He was erratic, but very eloquent; self-opinionated, but well versed in the Scriptures; and in literary culture and intellectual force was the greatest man among the early Mormons. After this the new sect strengthened and spread.

Joseph was a veritable Numa Pompilius in the frequency and fitness of the "revelations" he received for the guidance of his people in things great and small; and seeing that but few followers were gained by him near his home in New York, while many converts were being gathered in Ohio, he had a revelation that Palmyra was not a place for the Saints to prosper in, and he talked of the New Jerusalem in the West, and announced that it was time for the faithful to remove with him to *Kirtland, O.*

Smith has often been called the "American Mohammed," and Mormonism has been compared to Mohammedanism; and in many respects they *are* strikingly similar, although in so far as Mormonism resembles Mohammedanism it is true, as Dr. Jessup said before the Presbyterian General Assembly at Saratoga, it is only "a pinchbeck imitation of a putty original." In nothing, however, is there a greater similarity between those two religions than in their history. Both Mohammed and Joseph Smith were the subjects of fierce opposition and even persecution, and they both were compelled to flee for their lives. The Mohammedans always reckon their time from the " Hegira," or flight of the Prophet from Mecca to Medina; but while the Mohammedans have only *one Hegira* in their history, *the Mormons have four*. And, for convenience, we will consider their history under these four divisions.

CHAPTER II.

HISTORY OF MORMONISM (*continued*).

The First Hegira from Palmyra to Kirtland—The first Temple—Rapid growth of the Mormon Church—Brigham Young and other missionaries sent to foreign lands—The name "Latter-day Saints" adopted—Smith and Rigdon compelled to flee from Kirtland—*The Second Hegira*—The "Danites" organized—Rapid increase of the Mormons in Missouri—Jealousy of the Missourians—Mormons driven across the Missouri River by a mob—Their property confiscated—Their leaders imprisoned.

THE FIRST HEGIRA or exodus of the Mormons was from Palmyra to Kirtland, O., in 1831. This was a very tedious journey at that time, since they moved onward in wagons, carrying their household goods with them. On their arrival at Kirtland they were greeted by one thousand Mormons, who were the converts of Rigdon and other Mormon preachers.

Kirtland is three miles from Mentor, the home of the late President Garfield, and twenty-two miles east of Cleveland, and is situated in a remarkably fertile country. As soon as the Mormons arrived there they purchased a square mile of land, which they laid out in half-acre lots. In addition they bought a number of farms. They evidently expected to remain there a long time, since they erected a number of substantial houses, and a most beautiful temple, which Smith called the "School of the Prophets."

All Northern Ohio looked on in astonishment when the Mormons built their temple. It was, indeed, a remarkable structure. It was begun in 1832 and finished in 1836, the entire cost being $40,000. There was but little resemblance between it and the small meeting-houses common to the rural portion of Ohio; and although now it is over fifty years old, yet it is in good preservation, considering the neglect with which it has been treated, and might easily be restored to its former beauty. It is now owned by Joseph Smith, Jr., the son of the prophet, who, however, has no affiliation whatever with the Utah Mormons.

From the time the Mormons arrived at Kirtland they increased with astonishing rapidity, notwithstanding the fact that they were generally hated. Rigdon preached to crowds of people who flocked there from every part of the lake region to hear his eloquence. He seems to have had a wonderful power over the people, and so great an influence that it is felt even to the present day in that vicinity.

But the work of the Mormons extended beyond Kirtland. In the year of the First Hegira it extended over several of the States, and in three years afterward Mormon societies were established in Canada, Missouri, Illinois, Ohio, Virginia, New York, Vermont, New Hampshire, Massachusetts, and in nearly all of the Northern and Middle States and in some of the Southern States. A large number of converts were made chiefly through the earnestness and captivating eloquence of the Mormon preachers; for the more intelligent and better educated were sent out for that purpose. Besides, these missionaries had no compensation, and this was one secret of their successful preaching. They braved every danger and faced a frowning world rejoicing in tribulation. And then, too, the Mormons were a community who had all goods *in common;* and this fact threw a fascination over the new faith to thousands of uneducated people. They heard Scriptural expressions used by the leaders, but they had only a vague idea of what it was they professed; but still there was a novelty about the movement that captivated them, and they were willing to be led by insinuating men. Therefore the Mormon preachers won converts wherever they went. Rigdon said that Kirtland was only the eastern boundary of the promised land, and that from thence it would extend to the Pacific Ocean.

They were not content, however, to obtain followers only in our own country. In May, 1835, missionaries were sent to foreign lands to make proselytes; among the foreign missionaries was Brigham Young, who had joined the Mormons at Kirtland in 1832, and was ordained an elder.

Previous to this, at a conference of elders on May 3d, 1833, the name "Mormons" was repudiated and that of "Latter-day Saints" was adopted.

In 1835 Smith issued a command that the elders, who numbered between three and four hundred, "should seek learning, study the best books, and get a knowledge of kingdoms, countries, and languages." A professor of Hebrew was hired to teach that language, and a seminary erected, which is now used by the Methodists of Kirtland for their church.

The Mormons only remained in Kirtland seven years. Trouble had long been threatening, but it culminated in 1838, when Smith and Rigdon were compelled to flee on account of their bank bursting, with loss and annoyance to many sufferers. They fled to Far West, Mo., where the main body of their followers had in the mean time settled. This may be called the SECOND HEGIRA.

It was on this particular westward march that the

prophet organized a military command and a body-guard, and began to assume the prerogatives of his high military as well as spiritual mission. He had two hundred disciplined men-at-arms after he reached the State line of Missouri as his body-guard. They were called "Danites," and their conduct is said to have precipitated the tragic scenes that were followed by the expulsion of the Mormons from that State.

There had been some Mormons in Missouri since 1831 when Oliver Cowdery, one of the original members of the Mormon Church, was sent there to look for a fitting locality for the New Jerusalem, and, as they said, to evangelize the Indians and Gentiles generally. His report of Jackson County, Mo., was so favorable that Smith and Rigdon directed their steps thither under the greatest difficulties in travelling, making a portion of the distance of over three hundred miles on foot. On their arrival at Independence they were so charmed with the country that they at once selected it as the place for the New Zion ; and, to silence all cavil among his followers, Smith had a "revelation" to that effect.

The site of the temple was chosen with all the ceremony they could muster for the occasion. Here, Smith said, the Latter-day Saints would finally gather, Christ would appear in person, and the Mormons would reign a glorious and triumphant people for a thousand years.

Smith and Rigdon returned again to Kirtland and remained there until 1838 ; but meanwhile the Mormons increased rapidly in Missouri, settlements being made not only in Jackson County, but also in Clay, Ray, and Caldwell counties ; and with their habitual industry and thrift they made homes of comfort and rapidly gained wealth.

But while their general cause advanced, they were correspondingly hated by their neighbors. *Jealousy and politics* seem to have been the chief causes of this animosity. They had acquired so much property that the Missourians thought they would have "the rule of the counties" through their numbers and property. Besides, the Mormons were wont to boast of their political ascendancy. They called their prophet the commander-in-chief of the armies of Israel. They said that State would soon be in their hands, and finally the whole country. And the facts seemed to justify this braggadocio, as the whole of Jackson County was theirs, and converts were flocking to their ranks in great numbers. Accordingly, a public meeting was held at Independence by the alarmed Gentiles, which resulted in the Mormons being driven across the Missouri River by an infuriated mob into Clay and Caldwell counties.

With this dispersion the other Mormon settlements suddenly developed into places of importance, particularly a town called Far West. It was here that Smith and Rigdon came when driven out of Ohio in 1838. With their coming a new impetus seems to have been given to the Mormons. With all the vexations caused them by their enemies, mills, workshops, farms, and industries of many kinds sprang up in the wilderness.

With all these tragic circumstances there grew into a terrible reality one of those wild and romantic histories which could only have taken shape on a Western frontier, and which was developed by these unusual incidents, and by the vanity and egotistical spirit evinced by the Mormons. They claimed to be a chosen people under special divine direction. They shrank not from urging such prerogatives and acting upon them. They were the Saints, and all other people were Gentiles. They were the Lord's Saints, and the earth was the Lord's. They were led by an inspired prophet. Consequently, whenever the day of election for civil officers came, they must vote solidly the Whig or the Democratic ticket, just as the leader should indicate. It is obvious to any one knowing the fierce zeal of partisan politics how this course on the part of the Mormons would subject them to constant embroilments with surrounding citizens. Mutual acts of plunder and retaliation between the Saints and Gentiles became frequent, and they were terrible in their consequences. We must recollect all the while that the Mormons were the persecuted party on account of their eccentricities; and in a spirit of retaliation they in many instances drove their opponents from their immediate vicinity, burning their houses and confiscating their property. Worse than all, they drove some women and children into the woods, and two children were born of homeless mothers. This was the crowning event that fired the Missourians into a war of extermination against the Mormons; and in consequence the State troops were called out by the Governor, as he said, "to enforce order upon all citizens, even if it was found necessary to exterminate the hateful and obnoxious Mormons," *who were presumed to be in the wrong.*

A fearful drama followed under the leadership of Major-General Clark, who is described as being as rude as the most uncivilized of Mormons. He allowed the enemy to withdraw from the State, but he took all their lands and property to pay the cost of the war. The Mormon property thus confiscated was worth nearly two millions of dollars, and *that confiscation was undoubtedly an act of lawlessness and injustice.*

The Mormon leaders were arrested and put in jail, and at a court-martial it was decided to have them shot; but that act would have been so grossly unlawful that, on the protest of one of the generals, the court rescinded its orders.

With their leaders in jail, the Mormons submitted to the conditions of peace offered them, and prepared to withdraw from the State into Illinois, where Joseph Smith and his fellow-captives joined them after breaking from prison while their guard was in a drunken slumber.

CHAPTER III.

HISTORY OF MORMONISM (*continued*).

The Third Hegira—Sufferings of the Mormons during their journey into Illinois—An account of the murder of Mormons—Influence of this persecution on the minds of Mormons at the present time—*Nauvoo*—Its location—Its growth—The second Mormon Temple begun—Other public buildings—Laziness whittled out of Nauvoo—Internal dissensions among the Mormons—Political troubles—Smith nominated for President of the United States—Warrants issued against the Mormon leaders—Constable driven out of Nauvoo—Civil war threatened—Smith asked to submit to trial—Murder of Joseph Smith and his brother—Rigdon excommunicated and Brigham Young made leader—Consecration of the "Pride of the Valley."

THE *Third Hegira* or exodus of the Mormons was far more tragical than either of the previous ones. Twelve thousand Mormons arrived on the banks of the Mississippi River late in the autumn of 1838 in the most unhappy plight. Their houses had been burned, their fields laid waste, and they were nearly or quite destitute of every personal comfort. Every indignity which had been offered to the Missourians by the Mormons was returned with usury; and so terrible were their sufferings that the hearts of the Illinois citizens were so touched by their distress that they received with hospitality those who had travelled over the bleak prairies amid storms of wind and rain and snow. The aged, the young, and the sick had been alike houseless and homeless in the most inclement season of the year. Many who left homes of abundance died from exposure to the pitiless elements.

A Mormon poet wrote concerning these times :

> " Missouri,
> Like a whirlwind in her fury,
> Drove the Saints and spilled their blood."

And if we can look at this part of their history calmly and impartially, can we fail to see that Missouri's treatment of the Mormons was inhuman, unlawful, and impolitic?

A Mormon historian of these persecutions tells how twenty of the Mormons in the flight to Illinois, sleeping in a log cabin by the wayside, were shot dead through the crevices ; and after the massacre was over, a boy who had been concealed was dragged out from his hiding-place under a forge and shot, while his murderers danced around him. This historian further writes, after relating a number of such instances of Gentile cruelty : " We may forgive ; BUT TO FORGET—NEVER." And no wonder. Their treatment was barbaric, and to-day it is looked back to by the Mormons with just rage, and is used by them to awaken in the minds of their children the same spirit of hatred against a Government which has persecuted them from their very beginning.

When to-day it is said that the Mormons would not be molested if they would give up polygamy, they answer that those early persecutions took place before they adopted this doctrine. The fact is, that the mobs which attacked the first Mormons were made up in great part of the same low element that mobs the Salvation Army—a coarse rabble that, like a bull-dog, is ready to attack anything new. And as one nowadays hears a Mormon tell the story how the fathers of his people were driven out from their homes and forced to endure hardships untold and establish new homes elsewhere, if the hearer is not beguiled into sympathizing with the sufferers, he sees how the truly romantic story of those early days can fire the Mormon heart. He can then realize how many a young man who, for its own sake, would care nothing for his Mormon creed, will be ready to fight desperately for it in his indignation at the persecutions heaped upon his fathers. Thus, the remembrance of the persecutions through which their early leaders passed in Missouri operates as a strong power to support the zeal of the Mormons to-day.

After such trying and tragic events, their property lost and their health greatly shattered, one might suppose that the Mormons would have been ready to abandon their faith; but no, they were too strong in their belief for that. Their endurance was, indeed, *marvellous*. They clung to each other with great tenacity, and much pity was awakened in their behalf, because it was generally believed at the time that they had been treated with great injustice. Soon Smith was presented with a large tract of land in Hancock County, Ill., and immediately he had a "revelation" that this was the "centre spot," and he commanded the Saints to assemble there to build a city and a temple. The angel told him to call the city Nauvoo, which he said meant "*The Beautiful.*"

It was located on the east bank of the Mississippi River, forty miles above Quincy, Ill., and twenty miles west of Burlington, Ia. It was situated at a bend of the river on rising ground, which commanded a magnificent view of the Mississippi for many miles. The land given to Joseph was divided into lots and sold to the Mormons, by which he realized over one million of dollars.

The Saints from all quarters responded to the call to hasten to the new city, and it immediately grew in importance. The Legislature granted it a charter with extraordinary privileges, including the authorization of a military body, afterward known as the "Nauvoo Legion," a corps to which all the male Mormons capable of bearing arms belonged. Nauvoo became the capital of the world to the Mormons, and attracted general attention. It was changed from a desert into an abode of plenty and luxury. Gardens sprang up as if by magic, fragrant with the most beautiful flowers of the New and the Old World, whose seeds had been brought from distant lands as souvenirs to the New Zion; broad streets were laid out, houses erected, and the busy hum of industries was heard in the marts of commerce. Steamboats unloaded their stores, and passengers came and departed for fresh supplies of merchandise; fields waved with golden harvests, and cattle dotted the neighboring hills.

As might be expected, some adventurers, robbers, and people of a generally disreputable character joined the community to cloak their villainous deeds in mystery and religion. Speculators, too, came and bought property with the hope of large remuneration. These two classes of persons became the source of much strife among the Mormons themselves, and between the Mormons and Gentiles.

But, marvellous to relate, within three years after their expulsion from Missouri the Mormons had a prosperous city of 10,000 people, while near the city were at least 20,000 more, and in the whole United States and elsewhere they numbered about 150,000, *not much less than their present number.*

Soon after the city of Nauvoo had been laid out, the

selection was made for a remarkable temple which should be the crowning triumph of the wealth and perseverance of the Saints, all of whom were called to contribute to its erection by time and money. The foundation was laid with military ceremonies April 6th, 1841.

This unique building was made of finely-polished white limestone, and stood in the centre of a four-acre lot. It was 120 feet long by 83 feet in width and 60 feet in height. There were two stories in the clear and two in the recesses over the arches, making four tiers of windows—two Gothic and two round. There was a carved marble font resting on twelve life-sized oxen in marble in the basement for baptism. In structure the temple resembled no other church edifice, but was remarkably unique and graceful in its proportions, particularly the front of it, with its six fluted columns, its carved Corinthian caps and broad piazza. The walls were of massive thickness. The architectural ornaments of the interior were "holy emblems," and the spire upon the tower, which was 100 feet in height, was tipped with a gilt angel and his Gospel trump. Barnum, it is said, had this gilt angel in his New York Museum for years after the destruction of the temple.

The other public buildings in Nauvoo were the Seventies' Hall, the Masonic Temple, the Concert Hall, and the large hotel which the Prophet said was to be the "mission-house of the world," where he would entertain emperors, kings, and queens from the Old World, who would come to him to inquire of the new faith.

This city, although peculiar, had many *excellent features.* There was no licensed place to sell liquors, and drunkenness was almost unknown. It was well governed. All was order and peace. There was great thrift and industry among the people. Loafers or idlers were in disrepute. If a stranger entered Nauvoo and was found to be lazy he was at once "whittled" out of the town by the deacons. This whittling process was a very ingenious thing. It was a method by which the suspected person was followed by certain officials who surrounded him or his abode, and in unison whittled at sticks carried for the purpose. At first it might seem a matter of accident; but its continuance from day to day was too much for human endurance, and the undesirable stranger departed to the satisfaction of his tormentors. Perhaps it would be a good thing if we had some similar way of ridding ourselves of idlers all over our land.

But with all these good features, there were some indications of the purpose of the Prophet to introduce polygamy, although his sons deny that he ever practised it or even believed in it; but, however that may be, intestine quarrels on the subject of polygamy and other dissensions in the Mormon ranks served to bring on a crisis in affairs at Nauvoo in 1844, which resulted in the murder of Joseph Smith and his brother, and the expulsion of the Mormons from the State.

The real causes, however, were the same ones that operated against them in Missouri. The people in the neighborhood were jealous of the rapidly-growing and flourishing city. They complained that their property disappeared mysteriously, perhaps stolen by the adventurers and robbers who had joined the Mormons just to commit such deeds under a cloak, and for whose acts the Mormons, as a people, were not to blame. But the chief reason was political. Smith began to agitate the question of a restitution of the property they had unjustly lost in Missouri. He visited Washington and had an interview with President Van Buren, who said: "Sir, your cause is just, but I can do nothing for you."

The Mormons boasted that they had 100,000 in the faith throughout the country and that their vote was a balancing power. They voted in a body on all political questions. They even carried their arrogance so far in 1843 as to nominate Joseph Smith for President of the United States, and they have always declared that if he had lived until the next election he would have obtained that office. The Illinoisans, at any rate, believed that the Mormons determined to rule their State and intended to set all laws at defiance; and it was this belief that stirred their most bitter animosity; but internal dissensions among the Mormons gave them an opportunity to rid themselves of them in a most tragic way.

On account of troubles among dissenting Mormons, warrants were issued against Smith and other Mormon leaders; but the constable who served the warrants was driven out of Nauvoo. This act fired the smouldering hatred of the Illinoisans into terrible activity. The county authorities called out the militia to enforce the law. The Mormons hastily armed, and a civil war seemed impending, when the governor asked the Smiths to surrender and take their trial as the best means of satisfying the turbulent parties.

Now the charter of Nauvoo had been so cunningly devised that the State authorities were almost excluded from jurisdiction within its limits; and so the Smiths, feeling sure of an acquittal, obeyed the summons of the governor. They and other Mormon leaders were then conducted to Carthage and indicted for treason, and lodged in jail.

But on the 27th of June, 1844, an infuriated mob took matters in their own hands, decided to administer justice after their own fashion, and attacked the jail early in the morning. They broke down the doors of the rooms where the prisoners were confined, and horribly massacred Joseph and his brother Hyrum.

Now, those two persons were defenceless prisoners, and the Governor of the State had pledged to them safe conduct to the jail and before the court. Their murder was nothing else than *a most foul assassination*, the gravity of which was augmented by the fact that it was perpetrated by those who claimed to be upholders of law in contradistinction to the Mormons, who (they said) desired to set law at defiance.

But, besides being an act of lawlessness, it was the most impolitic thing that the people could have done. The martyr-like death of Smith threw a mantle of dignity over his person and a halo of consecration around his character that could in no other way have been secured; and it is reasonable to believe that, had Smith lived on, his own many weaknesses, the vulgarizing of revelation at his hands, the growing suspicions and disaffections of the faithful, and the fierce rancor and dissensions of the factions would have shivered Mormonism into pieces and sunk the fragments into depths too obscure for the searching of further history.

The Mormon people, with a self-control seldom seen, sought not to take into their own hands any measures of vengeance for the murder of their chieftain. After recovery from the first consternation over the awful tragedy, they began to ask themselves, Who shall rule the Church? Sidney Rigdon had already assumed the rôle of chief functionary, and had a revelation on this subject. But Brigham Young, who was President of the Twelve Apostles, hurried to Nauvoo from his mission in Boston; and by his shrewd sense, firm will, and practical ability he succeeded in gaining the leadership. Rigdon, who was accused of disaffection even in Smith's day, was excommunicated, and Brigham was triumphant. He was strong where Smith was weak—in prudence, sagacity, common-sense, and practical energy. These natural Cromwellian qualities he brought to the front and put and kept in force. He endeavored to heal matters between the Mormons and the Gentiles by pacific advice, but contentions waxed rather than waned. The charter of Nauvoo was repealed by the State Legislature in 1845, and Young gave out the edict that the Mormons must leave Illinois.

But, in the midst of these stirring and exciting scenes, the Mormons gave a curious exhibition of their faith in Joseph Smith. He had predicted the completion of the temple, and Brigham commanded his followers to remain in Nauvoo in order to fulfil the revelation of the Prophet. Unheard-of exertions were made to carry out this command, and the temple was finished to its minutest ornamentation. When it was ready, the Mormons flocked into the city from every quarter, and there was great rejoicing over the consecration of "The Pride of the Valley," as they called it. The interior was elaborately decorated with festoons and wreaths of flowers, chants were sung, prayers offered, and lamps and torches lighted to make it resplendent. When all this was done, the walls were dismantled, the ornaments taken down, and the symbols of their faith removed, to leave the noble building to be trodden down and profaned by the Gentiles.

Then began the FOURTH HEGIRA or exodus of the Mormons, the most tragic of them all.

CHAPTER IV.

HISTORY OF MORMONISM (*concluded*).

The Fourth Hegira—Young's shrewd plan of a Western Kingdom—Nauvoo's sad end—Journey of the Mormons to Council Bluffs—Young's forethought—The trip of "The Pioneers" across the wilderness—The halt at Salt Lake Valley—Young leads the remaining Mormons from Council Bluffs to Salt Lake—Their entertainment during their march—Folly of the Illinoisans in driving them out into the wilderness—Probable result of tolerance of the Mormons—Life begun anew in Salt Lake Valley—Salt Lake City established—Mills and workshops established and the Great Temple begun—Increase of the Mormon population—Value of their property in Utah—Public schools—A final brief glance at their history—How the MORMON PUZZLE will not be solved.

BRIGHAM long ere this had decided that his people must flee away to some remote region where collisions and conflicts should cease; and his sturdy will and untiring energy were exerted to carry out this decision. He selected California as the future residence of the Saints. At that time it formed a part of Mexico, and consequently was beyond the control of the detested Stars and Stripes and the uncomfortable people who had thrice expelled them from their dwelling-places. Brigham made known his purpose to the people and declared that they would move as rapidly as possible across Iowa to the Missouri River into the Indian country near Council Bluffs that season.

This new exodus began in February, 1846, the bleakest and coldest month in the year in that section of the country. An indescribable pageant of ox-carts and mule-teams, loaded with women, children, and all sorts of furniture passed out from Nauvoo to the miry tracks of the prairies; but the spirits of all, except the sick and helpless, were unbroken. Here Brigham Young proved himself the general as well as commander. He directed every detail of the evacuation. He arranged that the population should not move in a solid body, so as to disturb by their numbers the inhabitants of the sparsely-populated country they would traverse, but they should move in sections carefully selected, following each other at short intervals of time.

But in spite of this preparation there was a report that some of the Mormons intended to remain, and, in violation of the promises of the State, the Illinoisans called out the militia, and *drove the defenceless residents who remained from their homes at the point of the bayonet*, after bombarding the city for three days and nights. This was in the month of September, 1846. Thus ended Mormon history in Illinois; thus ended the history of Nauvoo, which is as wonderful as that of any city ever built. Its rise, progress, and destruction occupied only seven years, but many of its mysteries have yet to be told.

Meanwhile, Brigham was leading his companies across the prairies to Council Bluffs, their temporary halting-place. Men and women had been sent forward through Brigham's foresight to plant crops by the wayside for those who should follow to gather; but still there was terrible suffering and much sickness among these bands, who toiled onward obedient to their leader's direction. Dreams of a Mormon Empire, however, upon the Pacific coast consoled the people in great measure for the loss of the homes from which they fled and the hardships of their journey. As they moved slowly across the plains in 1846, the hopes which inspired them are well set forth in John Taylor's hymn, " *To Upper California :* "

> " We'll go and lift up our standards,
> We'll go there and be free ;
> We'll burst off all our fetters,
> And break the Gentile yoke."

Having reached Council Bluffs, Brigham then was compelled to make arrangements for the completion of the journey. The obstacles in the way of this intention would have intimidated a less courageous man. There was still about two thousand miles to traverse through an almost unknown country before the Pacific would lie before them. If at that time it was difficult to transport armed troops through the wilderness, what skill and energy must it not have required to send a nearly unprovided-for, feeble, and impoverished company of men, women, and little children such a great distance ? But his wisdom and forethought controlled the whole matter.

In 1847 Brigham and one hundred and forty-two pioneers pushed resolutely westward over the wilderness track for eleven hundred miles ; but while they were on their journey they learned that California had been conquered from Mexico, and that the Stars and Stripes were there supreme. They therefore halted on their arrival at the Salt Lake Valley, and Brigham Young, attracted both by the natural beauty and resources of that region, determined to make it the future residence of the Saints.

They arrived in the Great Salt Lake Valley July 24th, and, ever since, that day is the great day of celebration for the Mormons, eclipsing the Fourth of July entirely. These pioneers began improvements for domestic comfort and prepared as far as possible for the residence of the Saints who were still at Council Bluffs in sickness, poverty, and discontent. Getting matters into material shape, Brigham returned to Iowa, where his presence seemed to inspire the expectant Mormons.

In the spring of 1848 they started from Council Bluffs for Salt Lake ; and where in the history of our country will you find a more daring act than this of Brigham Young's? And where will you find a more heroic one than this of the Mormon people? Well has it been said : " It was a pilgrimage which has not been paralleled in the history of mankind since Moses led the Israelites from Egypt." They had sickness, weariness, skirmishes with the Indians ; but they also had their pleasures and rewards in this extraordinary journey of several months. They were surprised with beautiful scenery, and they languished over dreary wastes. Brigham told them stories, encouraged dancing to make them merry, and had theatrical performances to distract their attention. Children were born, and numbers died and were buried on the route, but they pressed on under their leader's direction for their new home beyond the States and their enemies, and in the autumn of 1848 crossed the Wahsatch Mountains and reached the Salt Lake Valley, their future home, although at that time a wilderness. Remember that this exodus was undertaken with the express purpose of placing themselves beyond the reach of the statutes with which their faith was in conflict ; but while they were journeying toward their land of promise, it was conquered by the United States from Mexico. Nevertheless, they were in a remote and uninhabited portion of the national domain, and where mountain barriers and leagues of wilderness lay between them and those whom they regarded as their persecutors.

Now, it seems to me that the Government and people

of Illinois did a most impolitic thing when they drove the Mormons from their State into the wilderness of the West. I firmly believe that if the Mormon Community had been allowed to remain at Nauvoo, free to develop its theories, in so far as they did not involve illegal acts, and in so far as they did, amenable to the law, but without illegal interference, the subsequent results would have been greatly changed.

Undoubtedly the best safeguard against error and its results is the influence of truth ; and the magnetic current of truth which mingles with the common-sense of the people in every circle of society in a land like this may be trusted sooner or later, without the aid of means outside the law or extra proceedings within the law, to prevent the propagandists of error, however they may associate, from doing serious damage to society. Had the Mormons remained in Illinois and been treated humanely, in free contact with the heathful currents of the life about them, the irresistible influence of a hostile public sentiment and of laws humanely exercised would undoubtedly have made the Mormon problem a matter of little concern. To assert the contrary is to assume that law is inadequate to the protection of a community from overt acts, and that the barriers of religion and morality are insufficient for the protection of an overwhelming majority against the contaminating influence of a generally despised minority. We think we are warranted in making the statement that the people and authorities of Illinois are in great measure responsible for the development of a structure whose abnormal features, destined to sure decay in that State, were driven to deeper root by persecution and to free growth by exile. It is certainly evident that *their treatment of the Mormon organization*, aside from considerations of Christian charity and humanity, *was lamentably wanting in political wisdom.*

But it is said they were a set of cut-throats and libertines, who should have been banished from all civilized society or cast in the depths of the sea. But that idea is doubtless a wrong one, and never had its origin in any mind except one full of prejudice. A picture, which we may unquestionably accept as a fair one, of the Mormon Church in Nauvoo was presented in the diary of the late Josiah Quincy, published in the *Independent* a few years ago. His dispassionate judgment did not lead him to the conclusion, so general in those days, that the followers of Joseph Smith were for the most part cutthroats, marauders, and libertines; on the contrary, while finding in their fanatical ardor that which opposition might develop into a disturbing element in society, he credits them with qualities such as temperance, industry, and thrift, which are among the most important essentials of good citizenship.

And, then, we invite you to look upon the thousands who poured over the Wahsatch Mountains and descended into the fair valley below. What think you of the *men* who have toiled with unmurmuring bravery for months through dangers of ambush and storm and flood on their westward way? Are these all pretenders and knaves, or the willing dupes of such? Does this theory, or the idea of lust suggested by the doctrine of polygamy (which was not announced until four years afterward, and has never been practised by more than a small fraction of the Mormon population), afford a sufficient explanation of the spirit which animates this multitude to espouse a common cause, to accept obloquy and exile, and to meet the perils of the wilderness in the face of approaching winter? In this stubborn adherence to a common purpose, in this fierce battle with adverse circumstances, in this devotion to wives and children, do we find evidence to warrant the belief that the aged men, the stalwart husbands, and the youth of this great company are moved solely or chiefly by the lowest and basest of aims ?

These hundreds of gray-haired *women*, too, in the passionless calm of old age ; these many mothers with patient endurance bearing their part in the struggles of this strange life and caring tenderly for their babes ; these young wives adhering to the fortunes of their husbands ; the maidens found in so many groups—are these representatives of womankind unreasoning bond-creatures or depraved women whose chief mission is to minister to the caprices and passions of base and brutal men ? Is all of this endurance of trial with a devotion approaching heroism the outcome of charlatanism, hypocrisy, and libertinism ? He who will answer these questions in the affirmative must be a blind student of nature and human history. No. To account for a movement like that which led 10,000 people into the wilderness, casting themselves upon the future with a wonderful faith and daring, requires an inspiration based upon something deeper and stronger than the altogether grovelling and mercenary motives which suffice to unite the fortunes of those who are only adventurers or knaves ? Yes, whatever may be said of the honesty or sincerity of those who moulded the belief of these thousands into its eccentric form, as they enter and take possession of Utah, they present the unmistakable evidences of *a faith founded on sincere conviction.*

Such was the beginning of the history of Mormonism in Utah, or DESERET, " The Land of the Honey-Bee," as the Mormons called it. Imposition upon credulity there doubtless was; ambition, charlatanry, and lust, each may be supposed to have had its place; but nothing short of a belief to which men and women gave themselves without reserve could have accomplished the results seen. And only this, taken in connection with the mistaken policy of the Government of the United States, can account for the subsequent marvellous growth of the Mormon organization.

Lands were at once surveyed and placed under careful cultivation, and Salt Lake City was made habitable. Settlements were established in every direction, the soil was subdued and irrigated for cultivation. The people built the city and began the temple and established mills, workshops, and numerous industries under the personal directions of the ever-watchful bishops. Missionary corps were newly organized for foreign lands, and an Immigration Fund established which soon resulted in a swarming influx to Utah from all parts of Europe.

The Mormons have increased in the last thirty years between five and six hundred per cent. The Mormon population of Utah from about 11,000 in 1850 had increased in 1880 to a little over 120,000 out of a total of nearly 144,000. In place of a wilderness we find a vast cultivated domain threaded by highways and railroads. The wild lands of 1846 in 1880 yielded a product in cereals of nearly two million bushels, and in precious metals a value of nearly nine million and a half of dollars.

In the year 1882 the total value of the assessed property of the Territory was $25,579,000. The public schools of the Territory, from the number of thirteen only in 1850, had increased in 1880 to three hundred and ninety, maintained at a cost of more than $200,000.

All these marvellous results have been chiefly due to the enterprise and thrift of a people expelled as outlaws from Illinois, and under the ban of the law during most of their sojourn in Utah.

This, in brief, is the history of the Mormons. And who will say that it is not wonderful and strangely unique? History, indeed, affords few examples of the growth, from such humble foundations, of a fabric based on a religious idea, so important and enduring as that which originated in the supposed revelations made over thirty-five years ago to Joseph Smith, an obscure resident in a country town of Wayne County, N. Y.

Born in 1830 of fanaticism and superstition; cast out from the place of its birth immediately after; driven in contumely from its refuge in Kirtland, O.; buffeted in Missouri, and driven to Illinois; baptized in the blood of the Nauvoo riots, and compelled to fly into the wilderness, and there developing into what it is to-day; with whatever contempt we may regard its origin, with whatever loathing we may look upon its accursed doctrines, it seems to me we are compelled to confess that there is something in the Mormon organization which demands for its adherents, in spite of its abhorrent features, a degree of respect and consideration. They should be given as much respect, at least, as we would give the honest Brahmin, Buddhist, or Mohammedan. Yea, more; for many even of their latest converts have been taken from our Southern and Western States.

They have had four HEGIRAS, or exoduses, in their history thus far; and many think they see indications, in the strong pressure of the law that is now brought to bear upon them and the temporary flight of some of their leaders, that they will soon enter upon another pilgrimage. And it is supposed that Mexico will be their next resting-place. But the Mormons are too strongly intrenched in Utah to be easily uprooted. They have too much at stake there to leave unless driven out by the point of the bayonet, as they were from Missouri and Illinois. But God forbid that this nation should do anything which would drive them beyond the borders of our land to infect the atmosphere of another! We can overcome this great evil in this land of light and liberty far sooner and easier than it can be overcome in any other land under the broad canopy of heaven. Nay, more; we are responsible for it. It was bred and born in our country. Yes, this iniquitous system sprang out of the bosom of the American nation; and *the American nation is in honor bound to grapple with it and throttle it.* The honor of the nation demands that it should be uprooted as speedily as possible.

But the fact is, that we are confronted with a powerful organization, a gigantic evil. And let no one suppose that a few words written on paper sent out from Government headquarters at Washington would destroy this system any more than a few words spoken authoritatively by Congress would destroy Romanism or Presbyterianism in our land. Many years will be required at the least for the effectual stamping out of the iniquities of the Mormon system. The great PUZZLE to solve is this: What remedies will be *effective* and accomplish the object *in the shortest period of time?*

In endeavoring to find the solution of this puzzle, we must regard this system in its THREEFOLD CHARACTER—viz.: as a *political* system, as a *social* system, and as a *religious* system. This we will endeavor to do in the chapters that will follow.

PART II.

THE POLITICAL PUZZLE.

"THE strange spectacle presented of a community, protected by a republican form of government, to which they owe allegiance, sustaining by their suffrages a principle and a belief which sets at naught that obligation of absolute obedience to the law of the land, which lies at the foundation of republican institutions."—PRESIDENT CLEVELAND.

CHAPTER V.

Mormonism a Theocracy—Manœuvring for office the cause of the expulsion of the Mormons from Missouri and Nauvoo—The "State of Deseret" formed—Lands illegally obtained—Brigham's movable house—Government officials compelled to flee—Federal troops sent—The oath of disloyalty—The Endowment rites—The American flag at half-mast—The control of the nation their aim—The political puzzle stated—Its causes—Necessity of Government action.

THE American nation seems to be slow to understand, and to all appearance is unwilling to believe, that the Mormon Church is A POLITICAL SYSTEM as well as a religious system, cherishing ideas and aims utterly alien and inimical to Democracy.

But, in the first place, it is *essentially* a political organization, its president being acknowledged as the supreme pontiff of the world, with both temporal and spiritual jurisdiction; and as such he is entitled to the implicit personal and unquestioning obedience of all Mormons. Mormonism is first and foremost a theocracy, and claims to exercise the only legitimate civil authority under the sun. It has no feature more characteristic and no purpose more fundamental or fixed than that of entire and undisputed temporal authority. In short, in its very nature and genius it is an organization transfused and overflowing with the virus of disloyalty and treason.

As early as 1833 Joseph Smith was openly accused of "aiming at monarchical power and authority," and in Missouri his followers inaugurated the practice, which has always since been followed, of voting solid; and this idiosyncrasy I have already stated was largely the cause of their expulsion from that State.

Then, crossing to Illinois and wild with schemes for kingdom-building, Smith's manœuvring for votes and offices was amazing. By trickery he secured a charter which made the city of Nauvoo independent of the Commonwealth. He was determined to be civil head of Nauvoo from the first, soon of the county also, erelong of the State, and eventually of the nation. His political game was played so recklessly for years that at length the fear and hatred of both political parties were incurred, and they united to crush the office-seeking hierarch and expel his followers.

Then they made their enforced exodus westward for the express purpose that, going beyond mountains and deserts, they might forever escape all interference from the wicked rulers of this world, and could set up the kingdom of God, with all its external forms. When they started westward Utah was not a part of the United States, and there they expected to be beyond the detested Stars and Stripes; but when they arrived there, much to their chagrin and disappointment, the flag of the free was supreme over all that region, it having been wrested in the mean time from Mexico.

Their plans, therefore, were completely shattered. Still they thought something could be done by energy and resolution; and so they made haste to set up a free and independent government, named "The State of Deseret," hoping that they would be received at once into the Union as a sovereign State. The modest (?) limits they fixed for their State included an area of about 700 miles square, or one tenth of the national domain. Deseret would extend from Oregon to the Mexican boundary, and from the Rockies to the Pacific, or over the whole, or large parts, of nine of our largest Territories.

Brigham Young was elected governor of this illegal Mormon State, some of whose illegal legislative ordinances were afterward incorporated into the Territorial statute-book; and for many years after Congress organized the Territorial government, this unlawful "State of Deseret" organization was maintained, collision between the two being prevented by the fact that Brigham Young was governor of both. The bogus State organization was the controlling power. Under its influence all sorts of arbitrary anti-American laws were passed by which leading members of the priesthood became the virtual owners of the mountain streams, the timbers, and the best part of the public lands. The right of the American people to these lands was ignored, and through the incorporation of some thirty-seven little villages in the rich valleys of Utah, more than 400,000 acres of the public lands were arbitrarily withdrawn from the control of the laws of Congress and appropriated by these priestly leaders. This was done for the express purpose of preventing those who were not Mormons from securing any of the public lands in Utah.

There is a block of 18,000 acres lying in the southern part of the rich and productive Cache Valley north of Salt Lake City, which Brigham Young secured by trampling the laws of the United States under foot. It is said that he had a four-roomed house built on runners. Hauling it to the centre of a section of land, each one of the four quarters would have a room on its corner. Four men would sleep there one night, each occupying a separate room ; and the next day they would make pre-emption filings at the land-office, while four other men would perform a similar act the next day and night; and so on, until most of the beautiful Cache Valley was thus entered. Soon afterward the men appeared at the land-office, paid over $1.25 per acre, and then they deeded the land to Brigham Young.

When the Government of the United States first undertook to establish a surveyor-general's office in Salt Lake City for the sake of surveying the public lands and disposing of them in accordance with the laws of Congress, the surveyor-general was given to understand that that country belonged to the Mormons, and he had to fly for his life. In 1856 all the representatives of the Government without exception had to escape from the Territory to save their lives, and were plainly shown that Americans had no rights in Utah.

And when, with a new body of Federal representatives, there soon came a military force under General Sidney Johnston sufficient to compel respect and obedience, Brigham Young cursed the Government, the troops, and the Gentiles, and in his usual coarse and emphatic style declared that he would "send them all to hell on wooden legs," and that they had better supply themselves then, when lumber was cheap. I mention these facts simply to show that the main object of the Mormon leaders from the very first was to establish a separate and independent government of their own, whose authority should be considered by the Mormon people superior to the authority of the Federal Government. And this accounts for the conflict which has existed between the Mormon authorities and the United States Government for the past thirty-five years, and which is still going on.

But not only does this hostility to our Government arise out of the fundamental idea of their religion as a THEOCRACY, and hence opposed to *democracy;* but also, and in great part, *because of their early persecutions in the States of Missouri and Illinois, and the unavenged murder of their chief, Joseph Smith, whom they regarded as God's greatest prophet.* The inhumanity, barbarity, and injustice that was meted out to them in their early history I have already mentioned; and in considering this perplexing puzzle, we must recollect that the Mormons have some cause for their enmity to our Government. *On account of wrongs done them, they are the sworn enemies of the Government and people of our land.*

They practise certain secret and mysterious ordinances known as "ENDOWMENTS." To the faithful Mormon these are made to seem precious initiatory rites whereby he is advanced in his knowledge of the true faith and exalted by the possession of new privileges. In reality they are a sort of crudely-acted religious drama, not unlike the miracle plays of the twelfth and fifteenth centuries. God and Satan, Adam and Eve, and others are persons in the drama. In its course there is a jumble of washings and anointings, of grips, and key-words and new names, and the investiture of each of the initiated in an Endowment robe. This sacred undergarment is always thereafter to be worn next to the person, carefully shrouding it at the last for its burial. There are also prayers and solemn promises and awful oaths, with penalties more awful, appended. It has been charged against these rites that they are scenes of indecency and licentiousness; but probably the charge is false. Absurd, irreverent, and even blasphemous they doubtless are, but it is to be believed not indecent.

Now, among the oaths there taken is one of resentful hostility to the American nation for not avenging the death of Joseph Smith or righting the persecutions of the Saints ; and thus the secret endowment ceremonies act as a powerful agency in ministering an unpatriotic, if not treasonable, bent to the Mormon system. Every Mormon who passes through the Endowment House takes an oath of eternal enmity against the people and Government of this land.

Yes, the fact is that there are 130,000 people in Utah cursing the American flag! And this was clearly seen on the Fourth of July last [1885], when the Stars and Stripes were hung at half mast on the Mormon buildings of Salt Lake City. Thus did they insult the whole American nation, and show their disloyalty in an unmistakable manner.

They are taught to be traitors to the Government. The children do not know the name of our President, and are told that John Taylor is their President. Many of the Mormons are scarcely conscious that there is a world outside of Utah. Salt Lake City is their Mecca, and John Taylor is greater than all the kings of the earth. They all believe him to be at the head of the Government, and that the laws are broken when his commands are not obeyed. It is flatly denied that the State has any authority over them, and it is expected that all Mormons will, if required, shed their blood in resisting the civil power if it interferes with their laws and customs.

The country at large seems blindly ignorant of the dangerous character of this institution that rears its insolent crest in the very heart of our country. The truth is, that in Mormonism we are confronted with an organized treason against our Government and our laws. Its spirit is that of rebellion. It will not down ; on the contrary, it is growing and spreading daily. The Mormons are penetrating Idaho, Wyoming, Colorado,

Arizona, Nevada, and Washington Territory. The income of the Church is about $3,000,000 annually, and is used in propagating the faith. Emissaries are sent to England, Sweden, and Denmark, proselyting the ignorant, and bringing them to our shores at the rate of about two thousand every year, to swell the number in their kingdom. One of the probable objects to be attained by the promulgation of the doctrine of polygamy was the speedier increase of their numbers than could be obtained in the ordinary Christian way. Their number in our land at the present time is about 150,000, and they openly boast of their power in politics. Recently Bishop Lunt, of Cedar City, Utah, in addressing a gathering of the Saints, declared : "We look forward with perfect confidence to the day when we will hold the reins of the United States Government. That is our present temporal aim ; after that we expect to control the Continent." And, after speaking of how rapidly the Mormons are spreading in the Territories and in Nevada, he said : " All this will in time help us to build up a political power which will, sooner or later, compel the homage of the demagogues of the country. Then, in some great political crisis, the two political parties will bid for our support. Utah will be admitted as a polygamous State, the other Territories we have peacefully subjugated will be admitted also, and then we will hold the balance of power and will dictate to the country. In time our sacred principles will spread throughout the United States."

That is their confessed plan, and in its execution they are shrewd and far-seeing politicians. No men better understand how to run " the machine." If any one takes the Mormon leaders to be fools, he is wonderfully mistaken as to their capacity. But while this is a shrewd plan from the Mormon standpoint, it seems to me that a great deal of alarming talk has been needlessly uttered about the fact that the Mormons are no longer staying in Utah exclusively, but are going into other Territories also and trying to subjugate them. The scattering of the Mormons would be the very best way to break up the evil which would result from their political power. If only the Mormons were to divide up, and companies of them go to every Territory, their political power would be broken ; for they would be but a small minority of the people of any Territory, and their votes would be neutralized. The only danger is in their being so massed together as to control by their votes the State or the Territory wherein they dwell; and the United States and the Territories should be on their guard so as to prevent their becoming a majority or even a large minority of the people in any one State or Territory where there are Mormon colonies at present. But it is not very probable that the Mormons will in the near future become the controlling element in any Territory or State outside of Utah.

The only political puzzle that we have *now* to unravel is in connection with *Utah ;* and it is caused by *two things :* The *first* is that *the Mormons are greatly in the majority*, the Gentiles numbering about 30,000, while the Mormons number about 120,000. The *second* is, that *the Mormons always vote solid.* If only their vote would be divided, as the Roman Catholic vote and the vote of other church organizations, the evil would not be so great ; but on account of the completeness of their church organization, the vote of all the Mormons is under the control of the priesthood. One need not study long to note how thoroughly and skilfully organized for power the Mormons are. *One will directs*, and by ecclesiastical communications and telegraphic wires the direction is speedily known unto the utmost limit of the land of their habitation, and promptly the entire massed body moves in the line directed. Petty offices abound in the system, and greater offices are rewards. There is, in fact, no organization on earth, unless it be the Jesuit, that is so well fitted as the Mormon to interest and keep loyal the members, to combine their faculties and forces, and to move that combination with efficiency and power whithersoever one master-will dictates. It is a mighty, terrible, solid pyramid, with John Taylor and his two counsellors for its apex; the twelve apostles come next; then the seventy, the patriarchs, high-priests, elders, bishops, priests, teachers, and deacons; then, last of all, the women at the base. Every fourth man is an officer; and as every member is sworn to obedience to the one above him, the result is that the head of the Church always casts the vote of the whole body.

In an article on "The Mormon Church," by Victoria Reed, in the *Bay State Monthly*, not long ago, it was stated as an illustration of the despotism of this institution that at church conferences there is never a dissenting voice, and at the polls always the same unanimous vote. Every Mormon has a vote to be cast as John Taylor dictates; and while the leaders of the Saints observe the forms of republican polity, their despotism is as absolute in its control as any on earth.

The great political *fact*, then, that we have to deal with is this: One of our Territories is in the control of a despotism, which defies our National Government, passively perhaps, nevertheless effectually, and scoffs and spits at its rulers.

THE POLITICAL PUZZLE is how effectually to wrest the

Territory from the hands of the Mormon Presidency, and establish there a Republican government in fact as well as in form—a government which will be in harmony with American principles and institutions.

Something, surely, should be done. The United States should not yield to this anti-American domination over so large a strip of her territory. She should assert her authority, and maintain it there as elsewhere throughout our land. Surely, those who say "*let it be*" are not cognizant of the *vast territory* which is now governed by the Mormon hierarchy. As Joseph Cook says: "The State of Vermont can be hidden away in one of the valleys of Utah and be no larger than a babe in a bed of full size." Utah has 84,476 square miles of territory; Vermont only 10,200 square miles. Massachusetts, with her 7,800 square miles, could be hidden away in one corner of this Mormon kingdom. Utah is larger than all New England, and about equal in size to the Empire State and Keystone State combined. Besides, its position is central, in the most important mining region on the planet; and also central in a group of undeveloped commonwealths, containing nearly a third of the territory of the United States. No; our Government dare not allow this Territory any longer to be ruled by an authority which is in deadly hostility to it, and sanctions what the law of the land condemns.

CHAPTER VI.

THE POLITICAL PUZZLE (*continued*).

THE POSSIBLE REMEDIES—The military remedy—The Government responsible for the situation in Utah—The disfranchisement of polygamists—Federal trustees for the Mormon Church corporation—Confiscation of unlawful funds—False statements about Mormons—Letters from the two Bancrofts—The dissolution of the Emigrating Fund Company—The Federal Commission remedy—The Woodburn bill, or Idaho statute.

THE question at once arises, What remedies should we adopt to get rid of this political evil—this *imperium in imperio*. The moral, the legal, and the military are open to our choice.

There are some who think that the evil is so great and the danger to our republican institutions so threatening as that there can be no adequate remedy short of THE MILITARY. Such a remedy, they acknowledge, would be severe, but the offence they consider as great beyond parallel, and the exigency most grave.

But for one I am an advocate of peace. If there is any other possible way of overcoming the evil, the use of the military arm should not be advocated, for it would necessarily result in numberless widows and orphans, and involve a heavy expense of blood and treasure. Bullets have no eloquence for the American people. The less gunpowder we can get along with the better. Our old wounds are not yet healed, and we are not hankering after a fresh fray. The order from headquarters which would summon the army to Utah would send a shiver through the heart of the nation. Suppression by force of bayonet is *the very last resort*, and we have not yet reached that point ; and God forbid that we shall ever come to that !

Besides, let us ask the question, Who is responsible for the present state of affairs in Utah ? We have already conclusively shown that the people and authorities of Illinois were responsible for their isolation in the West, since they drove them away from the surroundings that were calculated to modify, and finally to change, the drift of sentiment. Yes, it was on account of the un-Christian policy of the Illinoisans that we find the Mormons in a Western domain wide enough for a kingdom, and practically as far from the seat of authority as if responsible to a power beyond the sea.

And what was the policy pursued by the National Government toward them there ? In the light of the fires kindled at Nauvoo, it would seem that statesmanship would have discovered a necessity for the adoption of measures calculated to restrain the evil tendencies of Mormonism and prevent it from developing into an organization which must inevitably sooner or later bring it into open conflict with the laws of the land. But where in the records of Congress or upon the statute-books is there any evidence of the really serious and statesmanlike consideration which this movement demanded ? There were a people openly seeking a refuge where they would be free to disregard the popular opinion left behind them and to transgress the laws of the Government to which they owed allegiance. Were restrictive influences provided ? Did the Government guard against the realization of the boasted dreams of extended domain and self-government entertained by this law-defying people by erecting guards against undue encroachment on the public domain and by providing a government with the necessary machinery for securing the impartial reign of law and order? Were provisions made which would encourage the immigration into this garden-land of any portion of the law-abiding thousands who were landing upon our shores, and whose presence in Utah would have been a bulwark against and an ultimate cure of the evils of Mormonism?

The facts are the best answers to these questions. There was a total absence of wise legislation at the beginning. Afterward, laws were enacted calculated to suit the use of those whom they should have controlled. Then its laws and authority were nullified with impunity; and now we find a people of law-breakers waxed strong and maintaining an attitude of defiance to authority in the face of anathemas from the pulpit and the press, and a hot fusilade of ineffective enactments from the halls of Congress. This is the outcome of national legislation for Utah during the last thirty-five years.

In view of the facts, we venture to affirm that the responsibility for the present condition of affairs does not wholly lie at the door of the Mormon Church, and much less at the doors of those who constitute the mass of the Mormon people. Justice demands that the responsibility be laid at the door of the Government and people of the United States.

And, surely, fire and sword are not the instruments with which to cure the evils which our own supineness, want of statecraft, and mis-legislation have permitted to poison the atmosphere. A Government which is itself largely responsible for the evil it seeks to cure is in duty bound to consider well and act wisely in the application of remedies.

But while the responsibility of the Government and

people of the United States binds them to the application of a cure for the evils invited which shall not be intolerant or inhuman, it does not forbid the use of *effective remedial measures* suggested by political expediency and in keeping with Christian charity. Still, it is well for us to remember that we are bound as Americans to deal with this pernicious system on *American principles*, and as Christians to deal with it on *Christian principles*.

The only measure which has yet been enacted looking to the cure of the political evil in Utah was *the disfranchisement of the polygamists* by the Edmunds law of 1882; but although they have been disfranchised and rendered inelegible to office, they are only about 12,000 —a very small fraction of the Mormons; and practically the old men, the Mormon leaders, who have controlled the affairs of Utah for thirty years, have simply abdicated in favor of their sons. Consequently the Territory is still under Mormon rule, and the priesthood have it in their iron grasp. This law is good so far as it goes, but does not go far enough to effectually cure the evil.

But other and more radical measures have been *proposed*.

By the new Edmunds Bill, which passed the Senate on January 8th, 1886, it is provided that *the President of the United States shall appoint fourteen trustees to administer the property, business affairs, and operations of the Mormon Church corporation*.

There is no doubt that this act strikes at the root of the political evil in Utah, for the vast wealth of the Mormon Church in the control of the priesthood is the foundation of their power. Nevertheless, the wisdom, constitutionality, and effectiveness of the act are very questionable.

In the *first* place, if that law could be enforced, *it would open wide the door of the meanest kind of political jobbery.* It is the most delicious bit of patronage to which we have been treated for a long time. Fourteen gentlemen are to be rewarded for distinguished party services by the appointment to handle Mormon money. This is a new kind of party plum, and, in my opinion, is simply infamous.

But, in the *second* place, *there are grave doubts as to its constitutionality.* It is with much hesitation that we call in question the constitutionality of an act which is fathered by so conscientious a constitutionalist as Senator Edmunds and carried by a large majority in so conservative a body as the United States Senate. From *their* standpoint, perhaps, it is constitutional ; but from another standpoint it seems to be plainly unconstitutional. Congress is specifically prohibited from passing any law respecting an establishment of religion or prohibiting the free exercise thereof. The Mormon Church is a religious organization, no matter how false its religion may be. The Edmunds Bill places it under the care of the Government of the United States, and provides for the administration of all its temporal affairs. Now, if this can be done respecting the Mormon Church, it can be done respecting the Catholic Church or any one of the many Protestant establishments in our land. And who can doubt that if all the vast property, real and personal, of the Catholic Church were taken possession of by the Government, and its management placed in the hands of fourteen trustees appointed by the President—who can doubt that it would prohibit materially the free exercise of that religion by its millions of communicants in this country ? Clearly, then, the attempt to control the Mormon Church corporation by Government officials is contrary to the letter and spirit of the Constitution, and entirely foreign to the spirit of American institutions. If the United States once enters upon the business of administering church property, the Mormons may not be the last victims.

Besides, if Congress has the right to appoint trustees of a religious corporation in the Territories, then the State Legislatures would have the right to appoint similar trustees in the States, and there would be nothing to prevent a legislative body governed by infidels from putting all church property into secular hands, or a Protestant or a Roman Catholic legislative body from dealing in a similar manner with the trustees of churches of an opposite faith. And, therefore, we regard this proposed act to place the control of the Mormon Church property into hands antagonistic to its spirit as a most dangerous departure from American principles.

But, in the *third* place, *the act would, in all probability, be ineffective.* It is precisely what the rules of blood and iron in Germany under the inspiration of Bismarck attempted to do with the Catholic Church a few years ago. Bismarck said just what Senator Edmunds said : "We do not propose to prohibit anybody from believing in and practising the faith of the Catholic Church, but the Government of Germany intends to take charge of all its temporal affairs—to appropriate its property and administer it as we see fit to do." But there in Germany, where the power of the Government is absolute, this was found impossible.

And if impossible there, it will be doubly so here. Very likely if this proposition should become a law, and trustees be sent into the Territory, they would find themselves mere official ornaments without anything to do, for they would find no funds of which to take possession. The Mormons say that whatever property their Church has is owned and held, just as the property of the Presbyterian or Methodist Church, by the respective congregations. Formerly its property, real and personal, was held as that of the Catholic Church is—by a trustee in trust, and administered in the same way. The President of the Church, like the bishop, was the nominal owner, but held it in trust for the various congregations or parishes; but the Mormon Church authorities have determined that the property should be held and administered by and for each respective congregational or ward organization; and so you see that if trustees were appointed *they would likely find that the Mormon Church Corporation had no funds.*

Along with this enactment, there is another which provides for *the confiscating of the funds unlawfully gathered by the Mormon Church.*

Now, this act is not open to the same constitutional objection that the preceding is. It is a legal proposal, for only $50,000 can be held by any religious organization free from taxation; but its wisdom, justice, and practicability are very doubtful.

Its execution would be exceedingly difficult, so that not many honorable men would be willing to take the position of trustees of the funds which such a measure would remove from Mormon hands. The difficulty of separating the funds unlawfully gathered by the Mormon Church from those which justly belong to it would be very great, if not insuperable. Hence it would be very hard to defend such a measure from the serious charge of arbitrary interference with the rights of property.

It cannot be defended at all, unless it is put on the ground that the Mormon people, by continued hostility to the Government, have forfeited all political rights of every kind—even the right of property. It cannot be defended on the basis of justice at all. It looks to us to be a proposed theft in the name and under the authority of law.

But, as has been said before, in all probability if this measure should become a law, the trustees would find no funds at all ; for they could easily be transferred (nominally at least) to private parties.

Just here let me say that the people should be on their guard as to what they believe concerning the Mormons and the wealth of their Church. Charges are made that have no foundation whatever in truth, and small and trivial circumstances are so exaggerated and warped that they appear as crooked monstrosities, and are presented to the world as common Mormon occurrences.

A great deal that is said and published about the large amount of funds in the hands of the Mormon leaders, and the use to which they are put, has not a scintilla of truth in it, although the persons who publish it by word or pen, being misinformed, thoroughly believe it themselves. Thus, in one of the most reliable missionary magazines in our land, in May, 1885, it was stated on the best authority that the Mormons had a large corruption fund, and as a sample of the purposes to which it is put by them, it gave the following instance : " When Bancroft, the historian, was in Utah recently, he was told that if he would write certain things in his history of Utah, they would take two hundred and forty complete sets of his works, which would give him $40,000."

The writer determined to use that statement as *a test case*. He, thinking that the greatest American historian, George Bancroft, was referred to, sent him a letter of inquiry as to the truth of the statement, and the following was his reply :

THE POLITICAL PUZZLE. 85

"1623 H Street, Washington, D. C., February 3, 1886.

"*Rev. R. W. Beers, Elkton, Md.*

"Sir : Yours of February 2d is received. I am astonished that you should attribute to me anything so false as that I have been in Utah, and all that follows. You ought not to have needed to ask anybody about falsehoods so palpable.

"Very respectfully,
"George Bancroft."

But how should any of the great number of people throughout our land who read the missionary magazine where that statement occurred know that he had not been in Utah, and that the statement was false ?

Then the writer, knowing of another great historian Bancroft, Mr. H. H. Bancroft, the Pacific coast historian, made the same inquiry of him, and received the following reply :

"San Francisco, February 15, 1886.

"*Rev. R. W. Beers.*

"My dear Sir : In answer to your letter of the 8th inst., I would say that the Mormons never asked me to insert anything in my history of Utah, and never offered to take any copies of the work.

"Very respectfully,
"H. H. Bancroft."

The writer then directed an inquiry to the person in Salt Lake City from whom the statement in the magazine claimed to have been made, and asked him his authority for his statement. The answer was : "The Bancroft alluded to by me is H. H. Bancroft, the Pacific coast historian. His agent told me the Mormons had agreed to take two hundred and forty sets of his complete works in thirty-eight volumes, the gross amount of which (not the net amount) would be about $40,000, if he would publish a certain kind of history of Utah. Since Bancroft is a millionaire, the Mormon offer was not very tempting."

But H. H. Bancroft flatly denies that any such offer was made him, and the statement must clearly be pronounced untrue. And yet the person who made the published statement was one of the leading Christian men of Utah, desirous of disseminating nothing but the truth. He was misinformed, whether intentionally or not.

There is a deep-seated prejudice against the Mormons in the breasts of many in our land, which gives rise to many charges against them which have no basis of truth whatever. We must, therefore, be on our guard, and not believe quite everything that is published against them. Mr. A. M. Gibson, legal adviser of the Mormon people at the national capital, says that the reputed wealth of the Mormon Church amounting to millions "is all bosh;" that "the Incorporated Church of Jesus Christ of Latter-Day Saints is actually in debt to-day, and is a borrower of money." If that is the case, surely if the trustees were appointed according to the new Edmunds Bill, they wouldn't have many funds to handle.

Another measure to break the political power of the priesthood proposed in the new Edmunds Bill is to stop the importing of converts from abroad by *abolishing the so-called Perpetual Emigrating Fund Company and appropriating its surplus property to educational purposes.*

This seems to me to have not a scintilla of justice

about it. The emigration fund was originated by people who had been assisted to emigrate to Utah, dedicating the repayment of the money advanced to them to assist others in the same way. It was an entirely voluntary contribution. I cannot see what right the United States has to intervene to destroy an immigration company, if it is legally conducted, simply because the religious sentiments of the Mormons are obnoxious to the people of the United States. If anything is settled in American national life, it is that no man shall be called to account for his religious opinions. And so this proposed act must be an arbitrary interference with the rights of property. If Congress has the right to dissolve an Emigrating Company and use its surplus property for educational purposes, then a Socialistic State Legislature would have the right to dissolve a railroad corporation, pay its debts, and take possession of its surplus for the common benefit; and this, surely, is a socialistic doctrine which the great majority of the American people are not yet prepared to accept.

Besides, it would be *ineffective*. The attorney-general would doubtless find no funds to handle. The Mormons say that the emigration fund practically ceased to exist years ago. The emigration of Mormons now, they say, is the result of their own saving, with such assistance as their friends and relatives in the United States give them; and consequently, although the Emigration Company would be abolished, missionaries would continue to go every year to foreign countries and land converts by the thousands upon our shores and take them to Utah and other Territories to strengthen the power of the priesthood.

Even if all of the measures mentioned thus far as contained in the new Edmunds Bill were enacted, the great political evil now in Utah would remain. The Territory would still be in the hands of the Mormons, and consequently in the hands of the priesthood.

Another radical measure has been proposed, and was strongly advocated by ex-Governor Murray and many leading Gentiles of Salt Lake City, and was recommended by ex-President Arthur. The measure proposed is *the abolition of all Territorial government and the instituting of a government by a Federal Commission, appointed by the President, of nine persons resident in the Territory.*

It is claimed that, if this commission was composed of upright, patriotic, and practical men, identified as citizens with the interests of the Territory, they would give an immense impetus to business of all kinds and induce enterprising men to settle there, because there would then be an assurance that Utah was to be in truth an *American* territory.

Now, there is no doubt at all that that would be an *effective* remedy for the political evil in Utah. The only questions to consider are: Is it *lawful?* Is it *just?* Is it *wise?*

Senator Edmunds has declared it *unconstitutional;* and although there are precedents in its favor, yet its constitutionality may well be questioned. Certainly the Territory would not have a representative form of government under a Legislative Commission. The government would be an oligarchy.

Besides, not *all* the residents of Utah are disloyal in sentiment and feeling. There are at least fifteen thousand, and probably thirty thousand, loyal citizens; but the proposed plan confuses the innocent with the guilty, and so *cannot be defended from the standpoint of justice.* ALL are disfranchised, Mormons and Gentiles, alike.

And, then, it is *not wise*. The Mormons in all likelihood would not obey the local laws passed by such a commission, because they would have no voice in their making. They would not regard them as entitled to respect, and there would as a result be more internal disorder and disquiet than there is now, so that immigration of peaceable citizens would be checked rather than encouraged.

Then, it lacks wisdom when we look at the evil to be overcome. The political evil to be overcome is the existence of a non-republican government in Utah. The government now there, though *republican in form*, in *substance is oligarchical*, the real rulers being the triumvirate who constitute the First Presidency of the Mormon Church. The problem is, how to remove that unrepublican oligarchy and set up a republican government there as elsewhere. Now, see what is proposed! *A legislative commission of nine appointed by the President!* Why, the present government there is more republican than that proposed. The government now in existence is republican *in form* at least, and the officers are elected by the majority of the people and represent them truly. But the Legislative Commission would be not even republican in form. The people would have nothing whatever to do with their appointment—not even the Gentiles. That government would be thoroughly undemocratic both in form and substance; and even if it would truly represent the *Gentile* population, it would only represent a minority of citizens, and consequently would be undemocratic; for the fundamental doctrine of democracy is that the majority should rule the minority. As a proper substitute, then, for the present form of government in Utah, the Legislative Commission must be regarded as strikingly wanting. It does not solve the problem. It is unwise, inexpedient, and unnecessary.

Another law, which is far more just than the preceding, has been proposed recently by ex-Governor Murray (in his last official report), and was strongly advocated by Joseph Cook in his Boston Monday Lecture delivered February 8th, 1886. It was also introduced into the House of Representatives on April 1st, 1886, by Mr. Woodburn, of Nevada. It is known as the "Idaho Statute," because it has been in operation in the Territory of Idaho. *It disfranchises every man and woman who believes, teaches, or practices bigamy or polygamy, or who belongs to any organization or association which believes, teaches, or encourages the practice of bigamy or polygamy, and renders all such ineligible to any office.* That law would only disfranchise the Mormons, the disloyal element in the Territory, and would put Utah in the hands of the law-abiding citizens alone.

But it is open to the grave constitutional objection of interference with a religious belief. Those who simply *believe in polygamy* would be punished by this enactment; but our Government, whether national or State, has no right to inquire into *the beliefs* of our citizens. It is only when they carry their beliefs into *actual practice* of that which is contrary to the laws of the land that our Government can rightfully punish them or deprive them of civil rights.

CHAPTER VII.

THE POLITICAL PUZZLE (*concluded*).

Objections to proposed remedies—*Gladstone* on "Coercion"—A NEW PLAN ADVOCATED—*The Abolition of Female Suffrage—A National Colonization Scheme*—Natural resources of Utah—Superiority of the colonization plan over others—*The establishment of National Free Schools*—Ignorance the keystone of Mormon despotism—Public schools in Utah used for Mormon purposes—Proposed Federal Superintendent of schools in Utah—Territorial schools too few—Necessity of Government action—Prejudice disarmed by this plan—THE POLITICAL PUZZLE SOLVED.

ALL the measures that have yet been proposed are acknowledged to be unusual and extraordinary, and are advocated only on the ground of *necessity*, which William Pitt called "the argument of tyrants." It is said that the facts to be dealt with are unprecedented. An insolent anti-American empire has for years been growing in the body politic of this country, and it must be overcome *at all hazards*. But let us pause a moment. Is not that the great doctrine of the Jesuit—" *The end justifies the means*" ? That is an exceedingly dangerous doctrine to follow. No, fellow-Americans, we *must* not, we *dare* not, allow our righteous, passionate fervor against Mormon disloyalty to carry us so far as to violate fundamental principles of the American Constitution. Whatever we do, we must cling to the traditions of the past, and not depart from the spirit of our cherished American principles.

Besides, all of these measures are open to the objection

of *persecution* from a Mormon point of view. Threats of bloody resistance, especially to a Legislative Commission, have been made by Mormons even of quiet disposition. Now, if the evil can in any way be overcome without persecution, that way is by all means to be preferred.

Utah may well be called " *The American Ireland.*" Ireland is practically in rebellion against the Government of Great Britain, and she bases her rebellion on wrongs and abuses. Utah is in practical rebellion against our Government, and bases her disloyalty on the ground of injustice and abuse. Coercive measures have long been tried with Ireland and have been of no avail; and now Gladstone, the greatest living statesman, advocates pacific measures. When he introduced his Irish Home Rule measure into the House of Commons on the 8th of April, 1886, the most memorable day in the history of modern English Parliaments, in his great speech (confessedly one of the greatest efforts of his life) he said : " *Coercion, unless stern and unbending, and under an autocratic government, must always fail.* Such coercion England should never resort to until every other means has failed. The basis of the whole mischief is the fact that the law is discredited in Ireland. It comes to the Irish people with a foreign aspect." So we have tried prohibitory and repressive methods with the Mormons for thirty years, and they have failed. *They will fail to the bitter end.* The longer they are tried, the worse the result. They will only increase their enmity to the Government, heal over their internal dissensions, bind them the closer together, and wed them more firmly to their peculiar beliefs, which have made them objects of persecution. History can teach us that; and so we believe that it is time to inaugurate a change—viz., to work on the Christian plan, to overcome evil with good.

The plan which I have to propose to overcome the existing political evil in Utah and bring it into thorough harmony with our American institutions has the merit of being *in strict accordance with Christian principles and with American principles*, besides being, I think, *the most effective plan* in the end that could be proposed.

It involves THREE MEASURES, although the first is not absolutely essential and is advocated solely because it would greatly hasten the time when Utah would be redeemed—*i.e.*, the time when the majority of the voting population of Utah would be law-abiding citizens.

I. THE ABOLITION OF FEMALE SUFFRAGE in that Territory. This is one of the good measures of the new Edmunds law. I believe in female suffrage as a general principle; but I am opposed to it in Utah, as society exists there at present.

We acknowledge that this measure may from one standpoint be regarded as *unjust*. It may be said that it is unjust to punish the *women* by disfranchisement, and let the *men* go free, especially as they are far more guilty.

But, in reply, we say that there is no particular reason or justice in allowing the confessedly ignorant and enslaved women of *Utah* to vote, while the highly intelligent women of *Massachusetts* and *New York* are not allowed to vote. Until there is a Constitutional Amendment granting female suffrage throughout the United States, no American principle is violated by the disfranchisement of the Utah *women;* while the disfranchisement of the Mormon *men*, who simply believe in polygamy, would be in violation of a fundamental principle of our Constitution.

Then, too, it could not be regarded as a persecuting measure, for the *Gentile* women would be in the same category with the *Mormon* women.

Besides, one of the main reasons why we believe women should be allowed the franchise is that it would show a proper appreciation of their intellectual and moral worth; but in a Territory where the state of society is such as it is in Utah, where polygamy is proclaimed to be divine, and where there are no laws against bigamy, adultery, and kindred crimes, there can be no just appreciation of woman. Female suffrage under such conditions is a mockery and a delusion. Hence we advocate its abolition.

Now, see what would be accomplished by this measure, which is in thorough harmony with American principles! The Mormon vote in 1882 was 23,251 out of a total vote of 28,159. Of this vote, basing the estimate upon the number registering, the female voters were slightly in excess of one half of the entire number of Mormon suffragists. The disfranchisement of women would, therefore, reduce the total Mormon vote at least one half. The non-Mormon vote is now equal to considerably more than one fourth of the whole number of Mormon males of voting age. Consequently, with the disfranchisement of polygamists which has been accomplished, the non-Mormon vote would be nearly one third of the legitimate Territorial vote; and so by the abolition of female suffrage the problem would be reduced to this: How can the proportion of the non-Mormon vote be increased from one third of the total vote to a little more than one half? The answer to that question will obviously lead to the ultimate solution of this great Political Puzzle. This leads to the second feature of our plan.

II. A NATIONAL COLONIZATION SCHEME, by which large numbers of law-abiding citizens who are non-Mormons will be induced to settle in Utah *at once.*

This is the chief feature of our plan, and it seems to us the surest and speediest way to overthrow Mormonism, besides being a peaceable and Christian way. It is not a Utopian plan either, but one that is *entirely feasible.*

The material resources of the Territory are vast and varied. Its agricultural area is extensive and fertile, and parts of it are well timbered and watered. Within its ample borders abound mines of the useful and precious metals, as well as of coal and other minerals. It has more forests than Nebraska. It is true that irrigation is in some degree essential to successful agriculture, but Utah is not by any means the barren region it has often been represented to be. Most people think of it as a desert—a dry land, where no great multitude of human beings can ever find a prosperous home. But it has well been called *the American Syria.* Only let the soil have due irrigation, and it needs only to be tickled with the hoe, as the proverb says, in order to laugh into harvests. You may say the sage-bush, which is seen there in large quantities, is a mark of desolation; but irrigate the pastures covered with it, and you have bountiful harvests. As in Syria, when you irrigate the Jericho Plain you have most vigorous growths, and as on the plain of Gennesaret there were originally growths similar to the vegetation on the borders of the Nile, so to-day irrigation gives extraordinary fruitfulness to the cultivated lands of Utah.

It is true that the Mormon settlements extend to the full limits of the Territory in every direction, following the natural sweep of the valleys at the base of the mountains from north to south. It was Brigham Young's policy to occupy the best land as quickly as possible, but only about 500,000 acres have yet been occupied; and estimating that there are 2,000,000 acres, or the one twenty-seventh part of the territory, susceptible of cultivation (and this is a small estimate), there yet remain 1,500,000 acres unappropriated for future settlement. And so, notwithstanding the pre-emption of a large portion of the best arable lands of the Territory by the Mormons, there is yet a large and fertile acreage open for settlement. To ensure the occupancy of these wide and inviting fields by thrifty, sturdy settlers opposed to the disloyal and unlawful tenets of Mormonism, the laws relating to land-grants might be so amended as to prevent sales to those who are not prepared to prove their intention to become without reserve supporters of law and order.

But besides the agricultural resources, the mineral resources are also great. Whole tiers of counties are underlaid with coal, and the mountain ranges are impregnated in all their rifts with iron and lead, silver and gold. Until the completion of the Union Pacific Railroad the vast mineral wealth of Utah was untouched, the Mormon leaders being utterly opposed to exploiting the mines, knowing that their development would bring in a non-Mormon population; but since the building of the Union Pacific and the extension branches north and south, Utah has produced $50,000,000 in silver and lead, and its other mineral wealth, except coal and salt, is yet undeveloped. Ex-Governor Murray, in his report for 1880, said: "I know of no fact why it may not reasonably be claimed that Utah will prove the richest repository of silver, gold, coal, lead, and other minerals, of all the States and Territories of the West. Certainly no four hundred miles of mountain ranges have produced as many mines of immense yields and so many mining prospects as the suggestions of science and practical observation make those of Utah appear. Many mining districts heretofore inaccessible are now in close connection by railroads with the markets. Much of the ore, on account of its low grade, has not heretofore paid to mine ; but which now, on account of superior methods in extracting and reducing the ore, is made profitable. As a rule, the men who own the best prospects are not able to develop them for lack of means. Capital is needed, and with anything like reasonable business judgment can be made to realize most gratifying results."

Now, with such natural resources, what might not Utah become ? It is better adapted for general settlement than Nevada, and quite as good as Colorado, Arizona, or New Mexico. If its character and resources were fully and fairly set forth, it would present an attractive field to the hardy and adventurous emigrant. Rev. Dr. McNiece, of Salt Lake City, in a letter received from him February 19th, 1886, says : "This is one of the grandest and richest of all the Territories." Why not, then, encourage emigration thither of the right class ?

The Government might do much in this direction by offering special inducements in the acquisition of lands, as it did notably in the case of Oregon. Aid Societies, too, might be formed in the several States, as was done in the case of Kansas, when it was thought necessary to rescue that Territory from the grasp of the slave power.

There is already quite a large and powerful " Gentile" element in Utah, which has for years been struggling against Mormonism. They are faithful to the Government, and are generally enterprising, intelligent, and brave. Let their hands be strengthened. They would gladly welcome large accessions to their numbers and give to anti- Mormon settlers all the aid in their power in making favorable locations.

The work of colonization should be begun at once and upon as large a scale as possible ; and as the result of inducements and restrictions such as have been mentioned, it is safe to say that in a brief time the population of Utah would be surrounded with a battery of influences whose electric currents would act with irresistible force in hastening the establishment of a normal condition of things.

It is true that this plan would not immediately deprive the Mormons of control in the Legislature, but its effect would be to gradually introduce into it an element which would speedily make its power felt ; which would afford active support to the governor and his assistants ; and whose influence would soon divide the already dissentient Mormon elements, in so far as wise legislation is concerned, by winning the co-operation of the Radical Mormon Party, who are opposed to the union of Church and State ; and so it is admirably adapted to break up the power of the disloyal hierarchy. A wide discretion left in the hands of the governor as to the use of the veto power (although *absolute veto* power is a dangerous power to be vested in any man under a Republican Government), and the appointment to that position of a man of integrity and wisdom, would put it in the power of the Executive to defeat any attempt at improper legislation ; while in a few years the majority of the voters of Utah would be loyal, law-abiding citizens, and the legislative power would pass into hands perfectly safe.

This plan is entirely practicable, and is offered in the assured conviction that it presents the surest, speediest, and most peaceable method of solving the Mormon political puzzle. It does not transgress any American principle. It is not in any way unjust. And, surely, such a plan is far preferable to that of a wholesale disfranchisement of the loyal as well as the disloyal, not only as being more republican, but as being less likely to involve the Government in a long and bitter quarrel with a fanatic population. It does not take away any right (either the right of franchise or of property) from the Mormon people, who are now the majority of the citizens of the Territory. It could not, therefore, be regarded by them as an act of persecution. Hence it would not inflame their fanaticism nor increase their hostility to the Government; but it would tend to disarm their prejudice and animosity, for this plan would subserve their material interests by greatly increasing the value of their property. And while I do not think it would be the part of wisdom to admit Utah into the sisterhood of States until the majority of the voters are anti-Mormon, still I verily believe that by this plan, some time before that object would be obtained, many of the Mormons themselves would be on the side of the Government and would defy the political dictation of the priesthood. They could not mingle freely with a freedom-loving American people, such as this plan would surround them with, without very soon becoming imbued with some of their spirit of independence; and this would ultimately result in their breaking from the despotism of their ecclesiastical rulers.

But, as another step toward disarming the prejudice of the Mormons against the Government and breaking up the political despotism of the Mormon hierarchy for all time to come, we propose as

III. The third and last measure of our plan, THE ESTABLISHMENT OF NATIONAL FREE SCHOOLS all over the

Territory. Edward Everett Hale has said that America is to stand or fall according as she does or does not educate the South and South-west. Until the mass of illiteracy is greatly diminished in the Gulf States, and along the Mexican border (including all the territory acquired from Mexico), great trouble may arise at any time in the United States, from the collision of the uneducated portions with the educated. In view of that fact, Wendell Phillips once said that no thoughtful man could feel sure that *one flag* would rule this belt of the American Continent fifty years hence.

The education of the South and the South-west is the great task of the statesmanship of to-day. There are a hundred million dollars lying in our National Treasury, and we do not know what to do with it. The nation should take some of it and undertake the work of public education in the Territories; for while there is some objection to national aid to education in the States, as a needless interference with State rights, yet there is no doubt as to the right of the National Government to appropriate money for educational purposes in the Territories, since they are under its immediate control. The Government should begin educational work in *all the Territories* at once, and push it vigorously. Its future safety and welfare demand it.

But especially is that necessary with regard to Utah. The despotism of the Mormon hierarchy has for its keystone the superstition and ignorance of the people. If the Government would put a public school in every school district in Utah, it would undermine that despotism quicker than anything else. Give the Mormons light and education, and they will burst the bonds of their thraldom. The Mormon priesthood, well aware of this, take great pains to keep the people unschooled.

The public schools of the Territory are entirely in the hands of the priesthood, and, as a general rule, only Mormons are allowed to be teachers. They are scarcely worthy the name of schools; but, more than that, in violation of a fundamental principle of our Government, they are used for the propagation of religious tenets, and accordingly they become the means of instilling disloyal sentiments into the minds of the rising generation.

If Utah is to be thoroughly redeemed, it must be through proper influences brought to bear upon the Mormon youth of to-day; but the only loyal schools at present in Utah are those conducted by the Christian churches, which are far from sufficient in number. It therefore becomes the duty of the National Government to provide a loyal system of public instruction for Utah.

This could be accomplished only partially by making the Superintendent of Public Schools a Federal officer, as Senator Edmunds proposes in his new bill. The administration of such an officer, if he be properly qualified, and if he be supported by provision for the withholding of public funds from schools which instruct in matters of religion, and have also the power of vetoing the appointment of improper teachers, would so change the character of the schools of Utah as to make them efficient means for breaking down the disloyalty of the Mormons, instead of being, as they now are, a potent means for the propagation of Mormonism. But that is not all that is required.

The territorial schools now established are far too few to accomplish the desired end. The National Government should make an ample appropriation. It ought to put a public school in every city ward and every considerable village. It ought to equip them with the best appliances and the best teachers. It ought to fling their doors wide open to every comer. It ought not to teach any religion, Mormon or Gentile ; it need not ; but it ought to inculcate principles of patriotism and loyalty, and ought to teach the pupils to think and question for themselves. The parental instinct is stronger than a hierarchy. The appetite for knowledge is invincible, even by superstition. It would not be necessary to establish a compulsory system. It would be enough to establish a free system. The schools established by the different Christian denominations have proved that. Their Gentile schools are filled. The nation's schools would be crowded.

This would also go a great way toward disarming the prejudice and hostility of the older Mormons toward the Government. A great many of them are immigrants from other countries, who on landing in America were immediately taken to Utah ; consequently the Mormon immigrant has known the United States only as *an enemy.* It is time that we taught him that the United States is *his friend;* and in what better way could this be done than by establishing well-equipped schools for his children ? This would show that the Government had the interests of his family at heart. And we all know that there is nothing which will so soon touch the heart of a mother and father, too, as a kindness done to his child. Whatever prejudice or hatred there might have been before toward that person, after the kindness has been done to his child the prejudice departs and he treats him as a friend. So would it be if the Government would establish national schools of the best type in Utah. Many who are now its enemies would be its friends. Yes, put liberty and education in that Territory in the manner suggested, and liberty and education will solve the Mormon political puzzle. "We can let the

Mormons bring over their shiploads of immigrants unhindered by us, so long as they bring them to a community made free and enlightened. We can let them build their temple, so long as we overtop it with the school-house and the college. We can let them preach their superstitious liberalism, if we invite the ready minds of the oncoming generation to demand rebelliously a reason for the faith and the fear that are preached to them." Let the Government only grant a half million of dollars, and school-houses can be built and equipped everywhere. And to what better use could the money be put? It will not cost as much to buy books and pay the salaries of competent teachers as it would to dig graves in a war of extermination, and a far better result would be effected, with no blood spilled and no tears shed except tears of gratitude; for instead of heaps of men and women unnecessarily slaughtered, we would have A REDEEMED PEOPLE—redeemed from slavery to liberty, redeemed from disloyalty to loyalty.

We are firmly convinced that, if this plan were faithfully carried out in all its parts, less than twenty years would see Utah, with her rich harvests and vast mineral wealth being developed, and her million or more of people, shining forth as a bright star in the galaxy of American States, her people as loyal as those of Massachusetts or Connecticut—loyal to the very core; and where now the Stars and Stripes are cursed, trampled under foot, and placed at half-mast, they would then be greeted with loudest cheers.

PART III.

THE SOCIAL PUZZLE.

"PROCLAIM liberty throughout all the land unto all the inhabitants thereof."—INSCRIPTION ON THE OLD LIBERTY BELL.

"THE strength, the perpetuity, and the destiny of the nation, rest upon our homes."—PRESIDENT CLEVELAND.

CHAPTER VIII.

Polygamy only one of the Mormon social evils—Their social system *a system of bondage*—Contrary to natural law—Contrary to the spirit of the age—PERSONAL BONDAGE of the Mormons—Missionaries *must* go on duty—Dictation of the priesthood with regard to boarders and rents—Immigrants under their control—All members subject to Church orders—Power of the Church over daily business—Mormon mining contractors—MENTAL BONDAGE of the Mormons—Converts illiterate—The Mormon Church the opponent of free education—No independent thought—Excommunication of Henry Lawrence and others.

IF nine tenths of the people of our land were asked to denominate Mormonism as a social system, the answer that would be given by unanimous consent would be this: "It is a system of polygamy." And yet, after a careful study of the social condition existing among the Mormons, it is evident that *polygamy is only one of the social evils*—one of several branches from one parent stock, and therefore cannot be said to be descriptive of their whole social system.

One of the great political parties of our country has denounced slavery and polygamy as "twin relics of barbarism;" and that is undoubtedly true. But with regard to *Mormon* polygamy, it will be seen that *slavery* and *polygamy* do not occupy with reference to each other the relation of twin sisters, but rather the relation of *mother* and *daughter*. Slavery is the mother of Mormon polygamy and of all the other social evils of the so-called Latter-Day Saints; and therefore the proper denomination of Mormonism as a social system would be A SYSTEM OF BONDAGE.

It is consequently a system contrary to natural law as well as to the Christian conscience. According to Rousseau, the great French philosopher, man is a being by nature loving justice and order. In his opinion, in an ideal state of society each member would be free and the equal of every other—*equal* because no person or family or class would seek for any rights or privileges of which any other was deprived ; and *free* because each one would have his share in determining the rule common to all. It was these doctrines, taking root in the minds and convictions of men, that gave us our modern state of society, and that gave us our Nation, with its free thought, free speech, free press, and free institutions. The first public official document in which these opinions were clearly set forth was our "Declaration of Independence," which proclaimed that all men are "equal" and that "they are endowed by their Creator with certain inalienable rights, among which are life, liberty, and the pursuit of happiness."

The same views also formed the element of strength in the French Revolution. The first article of the "Declaration of the Rights of Man and of the Citizen," adopted in 1789, at the beginning of the Revolution, asserts : "Men are born free and equal, and have the same rights."

Indeed, these doctrines have been the source of all the social reforms of the past century. They are the guiding-star of modern civilization. They are the basis, not only of our Government, but also of our social system, which is one of liberty and equal rights. They are the spring of all noble thoughts given forth to the world and all the splendid achievements. To be majestic and ennobling, thought must be unrestrained ; to be praiseworthy, deeds must be uncontrolled.

In England the dominant party at present (June, 1886) is the Liberal Party, whose able leader is that "Grand Old Man," William E. Gladstone. Last fall, just before their great election, that party issued a manifesto of a very unusual character. It took the shape of a book entitled "Why am I a Liberal?" and contained definitions and confessions of political faith by the foremost leaders of the party. Among them Robert Browning answered the question in this characteristic sonnet:

> "Why? Because all I haply can and do,
> All that I am now, all I hope to be,
> Whence comes it, save from fortune setting free
> Body and soul, the purpose to pursue
> God-traced for both? Of fetters not a few,
> Of prejudice, convention, fall from me.
> These shall I bid men, each in his degree
> Also God-guided, bear, and gayly too?
>
> *But little do or can the best of us;*
> *That little is achieved through liberty.*
> Who then dares hold, emancipated thus,
> His fellow shall continue bound? Not I,
> Who live, love, labor freely, nor discuss
> A brother's right to freedom. That is why."

Those are noble words, worthy a noble poet. If he had given no other poem to the world, that would place him on the list of poets to be remembered by future generations, who are destined to be, if possible, freer than we. It is true, as Browning says, that liberty is the source of all achievements worthy the name. Horace Mann once said: "Enslave a man and you destroy his ambition, his enterprise, his capacity. In the constitution of human nature, the desire of bettering one's condition is the mainspring of effort. The first touch of slavery snaps this spring."

Since, therefore, this century is the century of progress, of grand and noble achievements, LIBERTY is preëminently its watchword, the ruling spirit of the age. The abolition of the negro-slave traffic, the progressive obliteration of class distinctions and race distinctions in law, the liberty of combination among laborers, the extension of the franchise, the limitations of the powers of riches—in a word, all our modern popular movements are only recognitions of the principle that each individual man is born with the right to regulate his conduct and pursue his ends in his own way, provided that he does not abridge the equal rights of his fellow-men. The principle of individual liberty has been the underlying principle of the social policy of the past hundred years.

But to this principle Mormonism is in the most bitter antagonism. It is true that it does not antagonize it openly. If it did, it would thereby strike its own death-blow. It claims to be in harmony with the spirit of freedom, and the official Church organ, the *Deseret News*, has for its motto, printed in large letters on its title-page, "*Truth and Liberty.*" Nevertheless, it tramples all freedom under foot. Its spirit is TYRANNY. A greater despotism the world, perhaps, has never seen. That of the Persian king in ancient times, and that of the Czar of all the Russias over his serfs in more modern times, pale in comparison with the absolute despotism of the Mormon chieftain and his two councillors. The condition of society in Mormondom is that of bondage, utter and entire. The constituent elements of man are body, soul, and spirit; and *these are all in slavery* under the social system of the Mormons.

Let us, therefore, consider this subject under these three heads—*personal bondage, mental bondage,* **and** *moral bondage*

I. **PERSONAL BONDAGE.**—Every Mormon goes through

the Endowment House, from which no man emerges with his manhood remaining. He has sunk to be the slave of the priesthood. In that house an awful oath is administered to every one, obligating the individual, under fearful penalty, to uphold the Church at every cost and obey it in all things. That terrible oath unmans the whole Mormon race and brings them into bondage. The Mormon leaders claim to be infallible—men inspired, who catch the very thought of God and pronounce His words. They are the direct vicegerents of the Almighty, and are at all times endowed by means of revelations with the wisdom to guide their people aright in all things, temporal as well as spiritual. This claim is admitted by all their followers. Accordingly, in the most tyrannical way the priesthood dictates about all the affairs of the people, telling them what store they must trade at, what newspaper they must read, what school they must patronize. In fine, Brigham Young claimed that his people could do nothing without his knowledge and approval, "even to the ribbons a woman should wear." The control of the Church over all the temporal affairs of the people is as absolute as their control of purely spiritual matters. One of their prominent speakers said a few years ago: "I cannot separate between temporal and spiritual affairs. The priesthood has as much control over one as the other." Therefore the Mormons are under *personal bondage*. Their persons, their services, their property—all are under the control not of themselves individually, but of their leaders.

At each semi-annual conference missionaries are appointed to go to the outside world and proclaim the doctrines of their religion. At the least calculation there are three hundred such missionaries constantly in the field, going up and down in the States of our own land, and also the countries of Europe and the isles of the sea. They must go at their own expense, and are required to stay until recalled by the priesthood. If it is necessary for a missionary to sell his last cow to get the means to pay his expenses, he must do so, even though his family should be left entirely destitute ; and he is taught to believe that the greater the sacrifice, the greater the glory in the next world.

A Presbyterian minister in the southern part of the Territory got the privilege of boarding in a Mormon family. As soon as the priesthood found it out this family was required to close its doors against the minister, although they were greatly in need of the money which he was ready to pay for his board.

Another minister in the northern part of the Territory hired a building for a mission school from an old lady connected with the Mormon Church, and paid a month's rent in advance. As soon as the priesthood found out what she had done, they brought such pressure to bear upon her that she went to the minister and urged him to give her back the building, although in her poverty she greatly needed the rent. Is not that slavery ? And yet President Taylor has stood up in the great Tabernacle at Salt Lake City and declared that they were in favor of the largest liberty for their own people and for all mankind.

Thousands of converts to Mormonism are brought from Europe to Utah every season, and this large immigration is under the complete control of the Church. It can be sent to any place it is thought best. If a colony is started in Arizona or Nevada, and it is thought best to enlarge it, the immigration is sent thither. The persons must go where they are directed, however much they might prefer to settle somewhere in the beautiful Salt Lake Valley, the Switzerland of America. Every settlement is made under the direction of the Church.

Not only is the foreign immigration under the control of the priesthood, but all members who have already settled either in Utah or elsewhere are subject to the orders of the Church. If the priesthood think it expedient to send a thousand or two thousand into Colorado or Arizona or any other locality, the number is divided out among the different wards, and each ward must not only furnish its quota of men, but all the means for the emigration; and the persons selected must go, although it is a great sacrifice to them to leave their cultivated lands and comfortable homes and go into the unbroken country of another Territory to again undergo the trials and sufferings incident to pioneer life.

The power of the Church is also brought to bear on all the daily business of life. In the mining districts of Southern Utah, the contractors for furnishing salt, wood, charcoal, etc., are all Mormon bishops. They hire the persons under them at starvation prices, and pay them in orders on the co-operative supply stores, in which they are either principals or partners; and the men so employed never see a dollar of cash. Should one of the common people undertake to do any hauling, wood-supplying, or other business with the mines, they would get an intimation that they must desist. If this hint is disregarded, a meeting of the Council is called, composed of the bishops and apostles; and as it is shown that some one of them is being interfered with, the order goes forth from the Church that this private enterprise must stop; and this no Mormon dare disregard. If one of the mining companies undertakes to do its business with any except the bishops, every obstacle possible is thrown in its way. Teams cannot be hired. The bishop pays wages at about a dollar a day, payable from the co-operative store; but if a mining superintendent wants men, he must pay four dollars a day. Thus the Mormon bishops secure all the profits of contracts from the mines. They take possession of all the woodlands and cut off the wood, never taking the trouble to comply with the law. They rule everything with a heavy hand, and woe to the poor man who dares to try to make his living independently. The serfs of Russia in the olden time were not more abject slaves than these people under the terrible power of the Church. Independence of action is entirely taken away from them. They are in *personal bondage*. Well may we exclaim: "Genius of America! Spirit of our free institutions! where art thou?"

> "Shall our own brethren drag the chain
> Which not even Russia's menials wear?"

But this is not all.

II. The Mormons are not only in personal bondage, but worse than that—they are in MENTAL BONDAGE.

Such tyranny as has been already alluded to is possible only because Ignorance and her handmaid, Superstition, are throwing their dark pall over the mass of the Mormon people. Mormonism grows mainly by imposition upon the ignorant and the credulous. Joseph Smith, its founder, was illiterate, and so was Brigham Young; and the mass of Mormons from the beginning were from a class of people whose education was very limited. Such also is the character of their converts now. They are gathered from the very lowest classes of the peasantry of England, Germany, and Scandinavia; and in our land the poor rural element of the Southern States, commonly called the "cracker" element, is a favorite and successful field for Mormon missionary labor, because the elders find as much ignorance and credulity among the poor whites of Tennessee, Georgia, and neighboring States, as they do among the low classes of Europe.

If you go into the Tabernacle at Salt Lake City, it is said, one is reminded, in looking at the faces of the people, of what we can see in Castle Garden. The marks of ignorance are stamped upon their very countenances. It has been aptly said : " The illiteracy of the average Mormon is denser than a London fog." In an article published in the *Presbyterian Review*, April, 1881, Rev. Dr. McNiece, of Salt Lake City, said that, so far as he knew, " after three years' observation in Utah, there are only three persons among the entire body of Mormons who can make the least claim to scholarship. One of these is a woman of notoriously immoral character ; one of the others is always spoken of as a religious monomaniac ; and the character of the third is such as to compel one to believe that he supports Mormonism simply because of the lucrative office which it gives him." According to the teachers engaged in the Christian schools there, the ignorance met with is simply appalling. In many cases neither men nor women know how to read. Children are plenty who never heard of God, and know no more of Christ than a beggar in the city of Nineveh in the days of Jonah. History and geography are to a great extent unknown and untaught ; even our own country outside of Utah is unknown. The Mormon leaders take great pains to keep their people in ignorance. Learning, intelligence, are everywhere at a discount.

The civilized world recognizes the fact that the

diffusion of knowledge elevates humanity. Shakespeare says :

"Ignorance is the curse of God,
Knowledge the wing wherewith we fly to heaven."

One of the chief features of this age is the desire for universal education, and every true reformer seeks to place it within the reach of all. *But the Mormon Church is the recognized opponent of free education.* Notwithstanding the fact that the Mormon priesthood has had control of Utah for well-nigh forty years, that Territory is the only one in the United States that has not a system of free schools, open to the poor as well as the rich. The teachers with few exceptions are young, untaught, and without experience ; and the schools are scarcely worthy the name. The main object of the Mormon school system seems to be to prevent the people from learning to think and acquiring information.

Now, why is this ? The only reason is that it is necessary for the Mormon Church to keep her subjects in ignorance to enable her to control them. This was the position taken by Brigham Young, and is the position taken by the hierarchy to-day. The plea of poverty cannot be justified, for the Church collects over a million dollars annually ; but this tax of ten dollars a year for every man, woman, and child in the Mormon Church is spent, not for free schools, which would develop manhood and fit the taxpayer to be an honorable citizen of the commonwealth, but for that which rivets tighter the chains that bind the people.

The minds of the people are in a condition of slavery. Independent thought there is none, and consequently free speech cannot exist. This is clearly proved, when we call to mind one of the brightest spectacles in the history of Utah. It was in 1869, when Henry Lawrence and his associates boldly stood up in the "School of the Prophets" and raised their voices in favor of free speech and free thought. A noble act of heroism that was—a stand for a righteous principle—a deed which should gain for them immortal fame, when we consider the real manhood it required for them to face such a powerful and tyrannical hierarchy. A noble fight it was on their part, but a losing fight; for they were at once expelled from the Church, branded with the stigma of apostates, their business was ruined, and they and their families were completely ostracized. That act of expulsion by the Mormon leaders is a clear proof of the fact that they are the bitter opponents of mental freedom. Who ever knew of any proposition being debated in their conferences, or any nomination voted down by the people? Who ever knew of any matter of interest being left to the people to act upon freely and unrestrainedly? *The leaders do the thinking.* They arrange all things. *The people must acquiesce and think as they do.* Is THAT LIBERTY?

Milton says :

"This is true liberty, when free-born men,
Having to advise the public, may speak free."

But free thought and free speech are not the prerogatives of the Mormons. They are MENTAL SLAVES.

CHAPTER IX.

THE SOCIAL PUZZLE (*continued*).

MORAL BONDAGE of the Mormons—Implicit obedience to the priesthood enjoined—*Crimes committed* at their command—Murders—The Mountain Meadows Massacre—Lee's confession—A Mormon carpenter's confession — Theft — Falsehood — Perjury — Why was polygamy promulgated ?—Why is polygamy practised ?

DEPLORABLE as the condition of the Mormon is, as already depicted in the preceding chapter, that is not the worst that is to be said of their social condition. They are not only in personal and mental slavery ; far worse than this, they are in MORAL BONDAGE. Sad to relate, their souls, their consciences, are enslaved, and consequently their condition is far worse than that of the negroes of the South before the Civil War. The central thought running through all the discourses of the leaders is obedience to the priesthood, and the consequences of refusing to obey counsel. It matters not how absurd the doctrine may be, or how much it outrages common-sense, if it is the declaration of the inspired priesthood, it must be obeyed ; and most of the people are so steeped in superstition and ignorance that they obey without question all orders from their chiefs, and even kiss the hand that rivets the chains that bind them.

The tyranny of the priesthood was well illustrated when one of the apostles on one occasion, while speaking in one of the ward meeting-houses about the solemn duty of obeying the priesthood, happened to look through the window and see a load of wood passing by. "Now I want you," said he, "to obey the priesthood so implicitly and have so much confidence in everything they tell you that if Brigham Young or any of the Twelve Apostles should tell you that load of wood is a load of hay, you would all say, 'Amen, that's a load of hay.'" Even though their very eyes should belie the statement of their leaders, yet they must accept it as true, because, forsooth, it came from inspired lips; and although they might be commanded to do that which their own consciences disapproved, yet they must do it, because it is a command given under inspiration, and their consciences are lulled to sleep by the Jesuit doctrine, "The end justifies the means." Surely, that is not religious liberty.

On account of this moral bondage, the worst crimes have been committed against both God and man, which have been laid at the door of the Mormon people, when in reality they were only the tools of the Mormon priesthood and the victims of an enslaving fanaticism. They themselves would not have committed them if they were allowed to do what their own consciences dictated; but at the command of the mouthpiece of the Almighty Himself they dared not disobey.

I. Thus, they have been guilty of MURDERS and ASSASSINATIONS for no other reason than that the hierarchy uttered their mandates that they should be accomplished.

Take, as an example, the *Mountain Meadows Massacre*, which is, perhaps, the darkest page in the history of Mormonism in Utah. It was a horrible butchery of one hundred and twenty innocent men and women who were emigrants on their way from Arkansas to California; and the dastardly deed cannot by any means be justified. For a long time the massacre was a deep mystery, and the Mormons asserted that it was done by Indians; but the mystery has been unravelled, and it is now known that that cruel deed lies at the door of the Mormon Church, the murderers being Mormons with some hired Indians, all led by John D. Lee, who was convicted of his crime and executed on the ground where the murder occurred March 25th, 1877, almost twenty years after the commission of the crime.

There were, no doubt, aggravations at the time leading the Mormons to the commission of the crime which we should remember. Ordinarily the Mormons were glad to see the arrival of Gentile emigrants *en route* for the far West, as it gave occasion for trade and barter; but at this time *Federal troops were advancing toward Utah*, and consequently a spirit of intense hatred toward the Americans and toward our Government was kindled in the hearts of the Mormons, and especially of their leaders. Their persecutions in Missouri and Illinois came up before their minds to increase their hostility against the Gentiles. Just then it was that there came within their borders this train of American emigrants. They regarded them naturally as enemies, and their very presence at that time was a powerful incentive to their extermination.

Moreover, these emigrants were from *Arkansas*, where only a short time before Orley P. Pratt, one of the first Mormon apostles, had gained his crown of martyrdom; and his murderer was not even arrested. Now the opportunity of avenging the death of one of their leading Saints was put within their reach, and this fact was another powerful inducement to commit the crime. But after all is said that can be said in extenuation of that terrible deed, it stands forth as *a most foul, shocking*, and *unjustifiable butchery*.

Brigham Young, as Governor of Utah, was in honor bound to protect those emigrants on their way across his Territory, and yet he was the author of their destruction. On the fourth day after the emigrants left Cedar City, in Southern Utah, about sixty Mormons, painted and disguised as Indians, it is said, left that place in pursuit of them. They were under the command of Bishop John D. Lee, and had all the equipments of a military force except artillery. Lee invited the Piute Indians to accompany him, and he directed the combined forces of the Mormons and Indians throughout the entire siege. At Mountain Meadows the victims were overtaken. They were taken completely by surprise, but they at once corralled their wagons and prepared for defence. For four days they fought heroically. During the third day's battle it became a necessity with the emigrants to get water. It was in clear view, but it was covered by the rifles of the Mormons. Hoping that the latter might have pity on children, they dressed two little girls in white and sent them with a bucket in the direction of the spring. *The Mormons shot them down.* The morning of the fourth day Lee told the men under his command that his orders were to " kill the entire company except the children." In order to do this, he used finesse and stratagem. He sent a flag of truce to them, offering to protect them from the Indians if they would lay down their arms. Putting confidence in his promise, they marched up to the spring where Lee stood, and placed themselves under his care. The line of march was then taken up, and after the distance of half a mile had been traversed Lee gave the command to halt; then immediately the command to shoot them down. All the men and women were slain, stripped of their clothing, and left without burial.

In 1859 General Carlton raised a cairn of stones over the bleached skeletons of the victims. Upon one of the stones he caused to be written : "Here lie the bones of one hundred and twenty men, women, and children from Arkansas, murdered on the tenth day of September, 1857." Upon a cross-beam he caused to be painted : "Vengeance is mine, saith the Lord, and I will repay it." Brigham Young ordered this monument to be destroyed, and said the inscription should have read : "Vengeance is mine, saith the Lord, and I *have* repaid it."

Lee was at length tried and executed for his part in that terrible butchery, but he was only the instrument of the Mormon leaders. He was in moral bondage, bound to carry out the wishes of his leader, however willing or unwilling he may have been to do so. He would never have ordered that massacre if he had not received an express command, nor would his troops have done the dastardly deed. *But they were in bondage.*

This may be clearly proved from the dying confessions of Lee, which were published after his execution. On the night previous to the massacre the Mormons held a council meeting. In describing that conference, Lee says : "I know that our total force was fifty-four whites and over three hundred Indians. As soon as those persons gathered around the camp, I demanded of Major Higbee what orders he had brought. . . . Major Higbee reported as follows : 'It is the orders of the President that *all the emigrants must be put out of the way.*' He then went on and said that none but friends were permitted to leave the Territory, and that as these were our sworn enemies, they must be killed. The men then in council knelt down in a prayer circle and prayed, invoking the Spirit of God to direct them how to act in the matter. After prayer Major Higbee said, 'Here are the orders,' and handed me a paper from Haight. The substance of the orders were that the emigrants should be *decoyed* from their stronghold and all exterminated, so that no one should be left to tell the tale, and then the authorities could say it was done by the Indians. . . . I then left the council and went away by myself, and bowed myself in prayer before God, and asked Him to overrule the decision of that council. At the earnest solicitation of Brother Hopkins, I returned with him to the council. When I got back, the council again prayed for aid. After prayer Major Higbee said, 'I have the evidence of God's approval of our mission. It is God's will that we carry out our instructions to the letter.' The meeting was then addressed by some one in authority. He spoke in about this language: 'Brethren, we have been sent here to perform a duty. It is a duty that we owe to God, and to our Church and people. The orders of those in authority are that all the emigrants *must* die. Our leaders speak with inspired tongues, and their orders come from the God of heaven. We have no right to question what they have commanded us to do; it is our duty to obey.' I, therefore, taking all things into consideration, and believing as I then did that my superiors were *inspired* men, who could not go wrong in any matter relating to the Church or the duty of its members, concluded to be obedient to the wishes of those in authority; I took up my cross, and prepared to do my duty."

From that confession it is clear that Lee revolted at the idea of the massacre, his conscience did not approve of it, and in committing it he acted as a slave, as a martyr, regarding it as a *cross*.

So doubtless it was with others under his command.

It is related that a missionary teacher asked a carpenter to make some repairs to her school-house. The work was done at noon-time, when the children were away from the school; and one day the man said, "I believe you are a Christian, and I want to ask if you think I can be forgiven for helping in the Mountain Meadows Massacre. I want to tell you; it is on my mind all the time; but if you betray me my life will be of no account." The teacher said she would not betray his confidence, and she believed, whatever his sins might be, they would be forgiven if he repented of them. The carpenter then told her how a lovely, golden-haired little girl was sent to a spring for water that dreadful day, and that he was one of those commanded to shoot her down; that her look of entreaty was forever before his eyes; and then the strong man wept at the remembrance, while making his confession, of a barbarity that he dared not refuse to accomplish. Was not that man in moral slavery?

Now, as that massacre was executed on account of the moral bondage of the Mormons to the priesthood, so also was the dastardly murder of Dr. J. K. Robinson in Salt Lake City in October, 1866, the murder of the Aiken party of six persons, the Potter and Parish murders, and the five hundred or more other assassinations which stain the history of the Mormon Church.

II. But not only has murder resulted from this bondage. THEFT is indulged in, not because their consciences approve it, but because they are taught by the priesthood that the plundering of all those opposed to them, whenever an opportunity occurs, is a duty, because whatever is taken from the ungodly Gentiles is that much put into the treasury of the Lord.

III. FALSEHOOD, too, is indulged in, whenever it will conduce to the benefit of the Church and shield her members from harm. A Mormon apostle, in an address at Nephi, Utah, cautioned the children, when asked how many wives their fathers had, to reply that they didn't know. "I'd rather have you tell a lie," he said, "to defend your friends and parents, than tell the truth, that will bring trouble upon them." The Mormons evidently do not pattern after the Apostle Paul.

IV. PERJURY is indulged in to a large degree at the command of the priesthood. Dora Young, one of the daughters of Brigham, apostatized and declared that the first thing that opened her eyes to the atrocities of Mormonism was her father's wholesale perjuries. John Taylor, the present President of the Church, has also set the people the same example. When placed upon the witness-stand, he has always been a very forgetful man, and could never recollect anything that would be of value in any case against any member of the Church. Such an utter absence of memory was, perhaps, never before exhibited in a court of justice. George Q. Cannon, also of the Mormon Presidency, the ruling spirit of the Mormons, said that he did not know whether any record of plural marriage is kept or not, although it is said that that book is one of the most important books they have.

Now, when the leaders commit perjury in that way, what can be expected from those who regard them as gods and as capable of no wrong act? And so we find that Judge Zane had to dismiss one case altogether, owing to the lack of evidence through false swearing. Women in polygamy have sworn that they did not know the father of their children. A daughter of Brigham Young professed on the witness-stand recently not to know that her sister was married, although her sister had had a child by her polygamous husband, and she had been in and out of the house frequently. Some time ago a Mormon mother was called upon to testify before the Grand Jury as to the marriage of her daughter to a well-known polygamist. The mother testified that she knew nothing about the marriage of her daughter, and denied knowledge of any facts connected with it; and afterward, on being questioned by one of her lady friends how she could swear to such a lie, she answered: "I only lied to their God; I did not lie to my God; and the authority justified me in doing so." Oh, what a picture of moral slavery does that present before our minds! The fearful oaths taken by a Mormon when he passes through the Endowment House require him to defend a member of the priesthood even by perjury, if necessary.

V. But that is not all, nor the worst. Under the head of moral bondage, I think, must be put that vice, which is called a relic of barbarism, and which has put Mormonism in antagonism to Christian civilization and the laws of our land. I refer to the practice of POLYGAMY, which is with many synonymous with Mormonism, but in reality is only one of the evils of that social system.

Mormonism had its birth in 1830. Polygamy was not promulgated until twenty-two years after, although Joseph Smith, it is alleged, received a revelation on the subject nine years before its formal declaration to the whole Mormon race. In dealing with Mormonism as a system, it must ever be borne in mind that polygamy does not form a part of the organic structure of Mormon society. It is an invention, recent in its establishment, and wholly an exotic in this country as well as in the countries from which Mormon recruits have been largely gathered; and it has been from the commencement to this hour an open and conscious defiance, not only of the public sentiment of the country, but also of its laws. It has known itself to be a transgressor, and every polygamous marriage has been deliberately contracted with this knowledge.

The question at once arises, WHY WAS IT PROMULGATED UNDER SUCH CIRCUMSTANCES? What was the object of the leaders in declaring it to be a divine revelation? While it may seem to many that polygamy is only an element of weakness in the Mormon institution, and destined to bring destruction upon the entire system, yet if we study the subject carefully it will be seen that it contributes strength to Mormonism in many ways.

1. In the first place, their numbers are increased much more rapidly than could be done by the monogamous system which is in vogue in our land.

2. In the next place, it gives a firmer union to the Mormon people, so that apostasy cannot occur so frequently as it did in Missouri and Nauvoo. By polygamy the Mormons are separated from all the rest of the civilized world; and as the world repels them, they are driven in upon themselves, to be welded closer together, to be mutual supports to each other under persecutions and trials. The unfortunate women who practise polygamy and the children begotten from it, even if they become malcontent, yet know themselves to be caught in a net from which they see no escape; and they remain in their place and practise, because, though their hearts are broken, their homes are saved by a religious sanction from foul disgrace. And even the thousands who are not polygamists (for not more than one tenth of the Mormons are polygamists) will uphold polygamy, because some near relatives, as sisters or daughters, are practisers of it. They, therefore, although not in polygamy, will yet stand up for it; and for them, too,

with the actual practisers, it becomes a bond, binding all together into a unity amazingly compact and unbreaking.

Having thus endeavored to answer the question, Why was polygamy promulgated ? let us now direct our attention to another and more important question, WHY IS POLYGAMY PRACTISED ?

Many suppose it is practised because it allows full sway to the passions of the sensualists, who are the only persons who practise it; but that is a great mistake. Some sensualists there doubtless are, who are polygamists, in Utah; but at the least nine tenths cannot be branded by any such infamous name. It is practised not because it is loved by the people and desired by them, but because they are urged—yea, commanded by the infallible priesthood to practise it. They regard it as the command of God; and that is the only reason why it is practised by ninety-nine out of every hundred of the polygamists of Utah. *It is because they are* MORAL BONDMEN.

Even Brigham Young openly avowed that when Joseph Smith gave him the order for the first time it was a great trial to his soul; and it is said that the locks of an apostle turned white in a single night when he was commanded to take another wife. The idea of taking a second wife to a man who is happily married is extremely distasteful. Polygamy, therefore, has enslaved the Mormon men, blunting all the finer feelings of their soul.

But if the men are enslaved by polygamy, the women are martyrized. A writer on Mormonism has said: "Whoever has read debasement in the women of Utah has done them injustice. Some there be who are devoid of refined sentiment and the nobler instincts of the sex, but no women in history ever deserved more respect and sympathy than the true women among the Mormons." They are taught to believe that polygamy is a divine institution; they are taught that it is their duty to make a self-sacrifice—to bear the cross in order to receive the crown. They are forbidden to covet the entire love of their husband's heart, because God designed to purify them from all selfishness and, besides, had commanded that if any oppose this revelation on "Celestial Marriage" they shall be destroyed; and while the Mormons do not use any visible coercion to draw persons into this complex marriage, yet that revelation, with its accompanying threat, stands like a frightful ogre, hanging over them like a doom, and sounds the death-knell to their happiness. The Mormon men have claimed that the women get accustomed to plural marriage and are happy in it; but that is a libel upon the nature of woman. Surely no woman ever desired to share her husband with another, and no husband could ever please two wives. No; the wives of polygamists in Utah are living martyrs. What days of silent grief and misery they must endure! The story of such women can never be told. Many a young wife has exclaimed: "I am fainting by the way; but for my children's sake I must bear up. What will be the end of all this suffering?" Many more have found early graves, the strain of mental anguish, added to physical labor, proving too much for their powers of endurance. In thinking or reading of such heart-rending sorrows, one is impelled to cry: "How long, O Lord, how long!"

And yet this moral bondage is suffered in this land, which is famed for its light and liberty. It is a shame and disgrace to our nation.

" How good to lead the nations of the earth
In every field of valor and of worth !
How good to hold the lightning in our hands,
And flash our energies to other lands !
How sweet erewhile to see the slave go free !
How dear to-day the breath of liberty !
How good to draw the larger, purer breath,
After the years of battle and of death ;
To feel how well our country bore the strain,
And settled back to rectitude again !

" And yet—and yet, just now a wailing came
Out of the West—our women steeped in shame,
The name of wife and mother made disgrace,
Home in our midst become the vilest place !
What if no black wrist feels the iron chain,
When snow-white breasts must bear the scarlet stain ?
What if the old plantation homes in ruin lie,
If Mormon temples proudly kiss the sky ?
* * * * * *

The day-break of true chivalry is now ;
And every knight is ready for the vow.
* * * * * *
How shall our flag, by Freedom's breath unfurled,
Greet Liberty enlightening the world !
Cowards ! The brazen image at a glance
Shall see the craven in each countenance !
The torch it bears in its uplifted hand
Shall not make light the shame-spot on our land.
Day-break indeed ! The midnight is not past.
Freedom, forsooth ! Not while yon temples last !
Enlightenment ! Our bitter inland sea
Gives back the word in shameless mockery !"

CHAPTER X.

THE SOCIAL PUZZLE (*continued*).

Reasons why Mormon slavery is maintained—Hope of earthly gain—Complete organization of the Mormon Church—Prospect of promotion in office as a bribe—Fear of earthly loss—System of espionage—Apostasy formerly punished by death—Mode of inflicting the punishment—Social ostracism—Religious conviction the mainstay of the Mormon social system.

HAVING already shown that the Mormon social system is a system of slavery so complete as to bind with its fetters body, mind, and soul—the entire man, let us now briefly inquire into THE REASONS WHICH CONTRIBUTE TO THE MAINTENANCE OF THIS DEGRADING SYSTEM, which is so utterly hostile to the enlightened and progressive spirit of the age.

1. There is, first, THE HOPE OF EARTHLY GAIN.

There is probably no system on earth which has a more cunning and complete organization than the Mormon Church. Supreme over all is the President, with his two Councillors. Then come the Twelve Apostles, who, in connection with the President and his Councillors, form a High Council, from whose decision there is no appeal. They may be regarded, therefore, as the masters in this system of slavery. Then come the Seventies (who are travelling missionaries), high-priests, elders, bishops, teachers, and deacons. One of the most cunning things about the organization is the large number of office-holders. There are over 23,000 officers reported as belonging to the Church—that is, one out of every three men holds an office either of honor or emolument. Each of these has a hope that if he is faithful to his masters he will be in time promoted. If any one of these 23,000 officers is disposed to criticise or become dissatisfied with the system, the office which he holds, and especially the prospect of future promotions, acts as a bribe to submission and acquiescence. Thus the hope of earthly rewards is one of the great sources of strength to the Mormon system, holding it intact.

II. Then, there is THE FEAR OF EARTHLY LOSS.

Hope and fear both operate upon the minds of the people, and cause them to submit to be bound by the chains of a tyranny whose equal can be found only by going back to the Dark Ages.

The Mormon hierarchy has a system of espionage, by which they are kept informed in regard to the feelings of all the people. The whole Territory is divided into twenty stakes or districts, each of which is presided over by a high-priest. These districts are again subdivided into about two hundred and thirty wards, each of which has a presiding bishop. The teachers and deacons are his subordinates, whose duty it is to visit each individual in their respective wards and find out all about his affairs, both temporal and spiritual. In this way, through all these various gradations, the leaders are able to put their finger on every man, woman, and child in the whole Church.

Before the Gentiles forced their way into Utah, and Government troops were stationed there, if any of the Mormons were, through this system of inquisition, found to be discontented and unsubmissive to the priesthood, inclined to free thought, free speech, and free action, he was soon taught a lesson by the "Avenging Angels" that silence is the better part of discretion, or that "dead men tell no tales." The Church held every man's life in its hand. Terrible was the punishment meted out for any offence or act of insubordination.

It is only a few years ago that it was the practice to inflict what they call *blood atonement* for any flagrant offence to the Church or any disregard of its orders. Brigham Young, after the people were well established in Utah, alluded on one occasion in a public address to the persecutions in Missouri and Nauvoo, saying that they always began with apostates and disaffected spirits; and then he said: "Do we see disaffected spirits here? We do. Do we see apostates? We do. I say to those persons, you must not court persecution here, lest you get so much of it you will not know what to do with it. Do *not* court persecution. Now, keep your tongues still, *lest sudden destruction come upon you. I say, rather than that apostates shall flourish here I will unsheath my bowie-knife and conquer or die.* Now, you nasty apostates, clear out, or judgment will be put to the line and righteousness to the plummet. Let us call upon the Lord to assist us in this and every good work."

President H. C. Kimball, in an address delivered in Salt Lake City August 16th, 1857, said: "If men turn traitors to God and His servants, their blood will surely be shed, or else they will be damned;" and this doctrine was put into actual practice. The culprit was never allowed an opportunity for defence. He remained in blissful ignorance of his danger, until at midnight there came a knock on his door, and he was ordered to accompany the four or five masked men that confronted him when he opened the door. Then he knew his doom, and so did his family, who knew they looked their last upon him. Being led to a secluded spot, a shovel was placed in his hands, and he was made to dig his own grave. He was then seized, forced upon his knees, his head held over the grave, and his throat cut from ear to ear. His blood flowed into the grave, into which his body was thrown and covered up, and no more was ever heard of him. His family dared not mention their suspicions, and no Mormon ever dared to be inquisitive or mention his name. Such instances were by no means rare.

Now the influx of the Gentiles has caused them to be more careful how they punish apostates or insubordinates; but we know little or nothing of the secret punishments that are still inflicted. The practice of blood atonement is now stopped by the necessity of circumstances. In the presence of thousands of Gentiles and Federal troops and Federal control, the Mormon Church dare not any longer enforce its commands by the pistol and the knife; but it has means of control none the less effective, which it does not hesitate to use. The apostate is now, it is said, handed over to "the buffetings of Satan," to be cursed in his business, in his family, in his body, in his mind, in all things that belong to him; and the Mormon priesthood have the will and power to see that these prophetic curses are fulfilled to the letter.

There does not exist upon the face of this broad earth a more complete social ostracism for religion than in Utah. Not many months ago a girl brought home some sewing which she had for a Christian woman. The girl looked round upon the happy home and burst into tears. Upon being asked the cause of her grief, she replied: "Oh, that I lived in a happy Christian home! You think me a Mormon, but I have *never* been a Mormon at heart. My mother was once the wife of a Presbyterian clergyman in England. About three years after her marriage my father died. I was the only child of my parents. My mother's people became Mormons, and my mother emigrated with them to Utah, bringing me with her. Here she married a Mormon, and I have been carefully taught in their religion; but I have my father's Bible, sermons, and diary. I know that his religion is true, and not this Mormon doctrine, which teaches of gods many, and heaven attained by sensual courses—women earning their salvation and exaltation in heaven by becoming the polygamous wives of some wicked man. I loath it; but I am poor. I can only do plain sewing for a living, and while I remain with my mother she will charge me nothing for board. I am not strong, and often sick. If I come out boldly and say, 'I will go to the Church of my choice and worship God according to the dictates of my conscience,' I shall be turned into the street, perhaps be denounced as a bad character—not an uncommon thing in Utah—and come to want. No, I must stop at home, be quiet, worship God in my heart, and pray for forgiveness."

If a man apostatizes who is in business he is no longer supported by the Mormons, and they in many places are nine tenths of the people. He is despised. He can get no work, since the Mormons control nearly all business contracts. The Mormon people will no longer hold intercourse with him. His family is the butt of ridicule and contempt, and his children are insulted and stigmatized. The entire family is as completely ostracized as though they had been convicted of an infamous crime. Now, it certainly requires strong heroism, real, sterling manhood, for one to face such a prospect for his family. Most people would obey the dictates of the hierarchy, whatever they might be, rather than bring such loss and shame upon themselves and their children. Thus it is seen how fear of earthly loss enters as a prominent factor in holding the Mormon people in bondage.

III. But lastly and chiefly, there is STRONG RELIGIOUS CONVICTION, which is the main prop of this social system. In discussing the Mormon puzzle in Utah, we must not forget that for twenty years this community was isolated by a thousand miles of barren waste from civilization. During this time it was literally a kingdom within itself ; and Brigham Young was king, his word law, his command a commandment from God. During that time the present generation of Mormons were reared ; and it is their strong conviction that the word of the priesthood is the word of God.

If we only glance at history, we will find many evidences of the great power of "Thus saith the Lord" over the minds of men. For religious conviction persons have burned at the stake and endured all manner of physical torture, to say nothing of the travail of soul through which they have passed. It is to this power, also, that Mormonism owes its strength. So strong is its control that the Mormons dare not, for fear of the loss of their soul's salvation, enter protest against any command coming, as it does, with these words prefixed : "Thus saith the Lord." The priesthood claim to have control of the "seals" and "keys" by which the gates of both heaven and hell can be opened and shut ; and they take the keys by which they pretend to open the gates of vengeance and rattle them above the heads of the uneducated and superstitious, until they are frightened into believing that, if they should disobey any edict of this priesthood, they would be consigned to the flames of eternal fire. It is this fear of the loss of their souls if they disobey, and the conviction that their leaders cannot command anything but what God has commanded, that is the strongest pillar that holds up their social fabric. Thus do the Mormon people with their own hands rivet the chains which bind in a fearful bondage their bodies, their minds, and their souls.

CHAPTER XI.

THE SOCIAL PUZZLE (*concluded*).

THE SOLUTION OF THE SOCIAL PUZZLE—Mormon slavery and negro slavery compared—The duty of the Government to break up Mormon slavery—The remedy the same as for the political evils of Mormonism—Brigham Young opposed to immigration of Gentiles—A growing spirit of restlessness—Necessity of surrounding the youth with an atmosphere of freedom—*Personal Bondage* of the Mormons overcome by Gentile colonization—Social ostracism no longer dreaded—*Mental Bondage* overcome by national schools and colonization—*Moral Bondage* overcome by the same means—This policy not to be confounded with the let-alone policy—An apparent policy of toleration—The alarmist's cry and its answer—The Mormon standpoint not to be overlooked—The cry of unconstitutionality—The proposed Polygamy Amendment to the Constitution—The cry of religious persecution—Imprisonment preferred to sacrifice of principle—Law impotent to break up polygamy—Supposed captivity of Mormon women a mistake—Mass-meeting of Mormon women to plead for polygamy—*Senator Hoar* on the solution of the social puzzle—How the law should be enforced and its probable effect—Superiority of the colonization plan over any other plan—Its effectiveness proved by the Oneida Community—*The Social Puzzle solved*—The duty of the nation, the citizen, and the Church.

IF our diagnosis of the Mormon social system is correct, then the only effectual remedy will be one that reaches the real evil, which is *slavery;* and as polygamy is only one of the results of slavery, remove the cause and the result will likewise be removed.

But this slavery of the Mormons is very different from the negro slavery in the South before our Civil War. The latter was a legalized traffic, and the remedy for it was *law*. The slavery of the Mormons is a voluntary one, and rests not upon law but upon religious conviction; and hence *law cannot be an effectual remedy*. The Mormon Puzzle, then, is a much harder one to solve than the Negro Puzzle before the war, and will require a longer time for its solution.

The galley-slave realizes his bondage, feels his fetters, hears the twang of his master's whip, and longs and plans for a release from his servitude; but he who is enslaved by a mental or moral dogma, while he thinks he is of all men the most free, is in the most fearful condition of slavery. This is the condition of all those who, like the Mormons, are compelled to yield a blind obedience to the teachings of an infallible priesthood; and it must necessarily be the case that all such are unfitted to discharge the duties pertaining to independent citizenship. He, and he only, is fitted to become a worthy citizen of our nation who strives to be an independent thinker, and who follows no guide but his own conscientious sense of right and wrong; but he, and he only, is a good Mormon who obeys counsel without question or gainsaying. It is, therefore, the imperative duty of our Government to break up this slavery among the Mormons, and to do it as speedily as possible. The Government is responsible for the growth of this system within its domains, and it is in duty bound to eradicate its evils so far as it lies within its power; but thus far the root-evil of the system has not been recognized. All the efforts of the Government have been directed only against one of the branches—namely, polygamy. The real evil is slavery, and it seems to us that the same remedy we suggested for the solution of the Mormon Political Puzzle is the proper solution of the Mormon Social Puzzle:

1. A NATIONAL COLONIZATION SCHEME, which would surround the Mormons with a people imbued with freedom, and exercising freedom of thought, speech, and action.

2. THE ESTABLISHMENT OF NATIONAL FREE SCHOOLS of a high order all through the Territory, by means of which the rising generation would be continually surrounded with an atmosphere of freedom. Nothing can change old Mormons, either men or women; but the young men and women—the rising generation—may be reclaimed.

The system of bondage in vogue in Utah can only be successfully maintained by its being isolated. The system thrived abundantly under Brigham Young, because it was entirely isolated from the rest of the nation. There were at various times individuals who dared to assert their God-given reason and freedom; but being alone in the Territory, they were soon silenced. But individual thought and expression have more encouragement now that the days of isolation have to some extent passed away by the opening of the Pacific Railroad and the mines of Southern Utah, and the influx of several thousand Gentiles. Brigham Young knew that the immigration into Utah of a large non-Mormon population would be the death-blow to his system, and so he used every means in his power to prevent it. He opposed most strenuously the opening of the railroad and the mines; but they were both opened by the aid of United States troops. In the same year that the Pacific Railroad was opened Henry Lawrence and his associates made their noble stand in behalf of freedom of thought and action, and against the dictation of the Church in temporal affairs; and ever since then there has been a growing spirit of independence.

Among the young there is a growing restlessness and an increasing sense of shame and wrong. The conditions are becoming dangerous, and the leaders see it. The American flag is overhead. The bombshells which issue from a free press are being heard and felt. Some flashes of the electric light of knowledge are to be seen, and some of the hopes which make jubilant the souls of American youth elsewhere are causing thrills in hearts in Utah which have heretofore been stolid. The thing for us to do is to surround them with an atmosphere of freedom, so that they will drink it in with every breath; and it will not be long before it will permeate their entire lives.

Their *personal bondage* would be overcome by their coming in contact with a people imbued with the true American sense of freedom. In a few years no fear of consequences would prevent them from asserting their rights. The tables would be turned, and woe to them who should deliberately trample their freedom under foot!

Moreover, by bringing in a large population of non-Mormons, social ostracism would not be dreaded as it now is. If the majority of the people were Gentiles, pecuniarily it would be to the advantage of a man in every way to break loose from his bondage to the Mormon priesthood. Think you that a man would work under a Mormon bishop for one dollar a day when under a non-Mormon he could double his wages? Think you that he would continue to allow the priesthood to swallow up about one half of his income when his income would be trebled each year if he broke away from their power? Surely not.

Then, too, the *mental bondage* of the people would thus be overcome. Even aside from the establishment of national free schools, the illiteracy of the people would be greatly overcome by the system of colonization proposed ; for a much more enlightened class of people would be brought in, and by contact with them the scales of ignorance to a great extent would drop from the Mormons' eyes, and they would see their bondage ; and to see it will be to break from it. Besides, the schools would inevitably be made free and greatly improved ; and the newspapers would be greater in number and scattered all over the Territory ; and who can estimate the power of a free press ?

Moreover, the *moral bondage* of the Mormons would thus be overcome. Even now, with only a small number of Gentiles in Utah, the Mormon leaders dare not command their followers to murder and assassinate as once they did ; and polygamy would be more effectually overcome in that way than in any other.

But the policy which I here advocate must not be confounded with the let-alone policy which has been advocated by some, but which is a policy which no true lover of humanity, if he knows the enormity of the existing evils of the system, can hold for a moment. It was that policy which has caused the system to attain its present rank growth. It was that policy which has brought disgrace upon our nation in the eyes of the civilized world. Shame that it should be held by any American ! Was it the let-alone policy by which the awful oppression of the priesthood was first broken in England by that immortal hero and champion of liberty, John Wicliffe ? Was that the way in which Luther brought deliverance to the oppressed thousands of Germany, and Knox established civil and religious freedom upon the shattered ruins of priestly corruption and tyranny among Scotland's hills and vales ? The let-alone policy was tried in our land with negro slavery for more than a hundred years. Did it die out? Let the answer come from the half million graves where sleep the unreturning heroes of the Blue and the Gray.

Accordingly, the policy which I advocate is not the let-alone policy. Far from it. It is rather the antipodes of that policy, the furthest remove from it possible. Instead of letting every Mormon alone in his voluntary bondage, *it touches every Mormon;* it brings a power to bear upon every one which he cannot help but feel. It brings him into personal contact with the spirit of freedom as it is exemplified in the genuine American.

True, it may be called a policy of toleration; but therein lies its strength and its superiority over any purely repressive policy, for it is regarded as an axiom that to tolerate error where truth surrounds it is the best means for its destruction. The evils in the Mormon system would long ago have been sunk out of sight but for its isolation from vital contact with truth. What the result of a battle between Truth and Error will be is known to all; but to conquer, Truth must be brought into close contact with Error. The trouble has been that Utah until quite recently has been hedged in by a Chinese wall of separation, so that Truth and Liberty have been shut out. The plan we advocate breaks down this Chinese wall entirely, and lets in the light of Truth and Liberty upon every Mormon soul. It allows Truth to have free course and fair play. There will then be a hand-to-hand combat between Truth and Error; and who can doubt as to the result? "*Truth is mighty and will prevail.*"

But some alarmist may cry: "Ah! but it will take time for that moral battle to be fought out to the end, and in the mean time the horrid cancer will spread and spread, and even our own families will not be safe from its infection."

But, in reply, it can be said that nothing short of the annihilation of the Mormons would overcome polygamy very soon. Even at the shortest, it will take several years to accomplish its effectual overthrow. The Utah Commission, in their report to the Secretary of the Interior, September 24th, 1886, deemed it proper to reiterate on this point what they had before said in their report for 1884, viz. :

"As the Government has to deal here with a people who are wonderfully superstitious and fanatically devoted to their system of religion, the public should not expect, as the immediate result of the present laws of Congress, nor indeed of any legislation, however radical, the sudden overthrow of polygamy; and the most that can be predicted of such legislation is, that it will, if no step backward be taken, soon ameliorate the harder conditions of Mormonism, and hasten the day for its final extinction."

Furthermore, the cry that "even our own families will not be safe from the infection of this ever-spreading cancer" is nothing but sheer cant—such a cry as the ranting demagogue might raise; and it only shows how ignorant most people are in regard to this question of Mormonism, even those who claim to understand it. Polygamy is not taught by the Mormon missionaries, and is not practised outside of Utah, and is practised there only by a small minority of the people. In the letter of the First Presidency to the Mormons at their semi-annual conference, dated October 6th, 1885, there were the following statements, coming from the head of the Church, and which are known to be true : "We never have believed or taught that the doctrine of celestial marriage was designed for universal practice. . . . There appears to be a fallacious idea abroad regarding this doctrine. It has been asserted that there was a design to propagate it outside of our community, and thus introduce into the United States an element opposed to the Christian views of this and other nations. On the contrary, our elders have been instructed not to introduce the practice of that principle anywhere outside of the gathering-place of the Saints; and they do not preach it abroad to any extent, even in theory, except on occasions when it is called for or when they are assailed on account of it. . . . It should also be understood that the practice is not generally admissible even among the Latter-Day Saints. It is strictly guarded, the intention being to allow only those who are above reproach to enter into the relationship. . . . The idea, therefore, that plural marriage is a menace to the general monogamous system is without foundation. This fallacy is further exhibited by the fact of the popular antipathy with which it is regarded, people outside of our Church exhibiting a disposition the reverse of favorable to its establishment in other communities, making the extension of its practice abroad impossible." No; our own homes are not in much danger from this evil. The Mormons in Utah will be the only sufferers. There should be no selfish motive aroused for the destruction of this evil. Neither we nor our families are in great danger. Honor and humanity are the motives which should actuate every American to wipe out this foul blot upon our nation's face and to uplift our brethren from the degradation and bondage of this accursed system; and although the plan with which we propose to accomplish this end will take some few years before the climax will be reached, yet while the plan is gradually being wrought out it will place a greater check upon the evil than any other plan, and in the end will be effectual in breaking it up, which cannot be said of any other plan yet proposed. And what is more, it would accomplish the end with less of bitter spirit being manifested and with less property and lives lost than any other plan that could possibly be brought forth, because it is in strict accord with Christian principles and has nothing in connection with it which could be construed by the Mormons as *religious persecution*.

In dealing with this question we must not overlook the Mormon standpoint, although it may differ from our own. The law against polygamy is regarded by the Mormons, in the first place, as *unconstitutional*. The existing prohibitory law is only a statute-law, which they claim to be out of harmony with the fundamental law of our land as expressed in the Constitution. The latter they claim to revere as inspired. Accordingly, their constant hope and effort is to obtain admission into the Union as a State, so that they might no longer be under the exclusive control of Congress. Under the Constitution as it now is, Congress has no legislative jurisdiction over the question of polygamy in the different States of the Union. The whole subject, together with that of marriage and divorce, is left with the States themselves, and may be regulated by them according to their own discretion. Knowing this, the Mormons are working strenuously to have Utah admitted as a State with all its rights and privileges; then they could bid defiance to all the statute-laws of Congress on the subject of polygamy, and in the exercise of their undoubted right they would enact a law allowing polygamy, which would not transgress any article of our Constitution. The earnest efforts of the Mormons will naturally be directed to that end as long as the Constitution remains as it is. The proper thing to do in order to completely overthrow that idea among the Mormons is to pass the proposed *Polygamy Amendment* to the Constitution. The Mormons would then see that, so far as that institution is concerned, they have nothing to gain by gaining political control of a State. No State could establish polygamy, any more than it could establish slavery; and if any State, owing to local public sentiment or partisan politics, were remiss in dealing with polygamists, the general Government would have power to supply the remedy. If such an amendment were made to the Constitution, the cry of the Mormons concerning the unconstitutionality of the Anti-Polygamy Law would be completely overcome; for, as the Utah Commission very aptly say in their report for 1886, "they would probably not have the hardihood to say that *the Constitution itself is unconstitutional*, and it is not unreasonable to predict that the more sagacious and influential persons among the Mormons would realize the hopelessness of a further conflict with the Government, and accommodate themselves to the inevitable by the exercise of that 'worldly wisdom' which so often tempers and modifies the conduct of religious fanatics."

Nevertheless, the Mormons could still raise their greatest cry—that which has the greatest weight with them—the cry of *religious persecution;* because then, as now, they would claim that the law interfered with their religion. We cannot admit the truth of their assertion. Chief-Justice Waite was right when he delivered the opinion of the United States Supreme Court on this subject: " Laws are made for the government of actions; and while they cannot interfere with mere religious belief and opinions, they may with practices. Suppose one believed that human sacrifices were a necessary part of religious worship, would it be seriously contended that the civil government under which we lived could not interfere to prevent the sacrifice? Or if a wife religiously believed it was her duty to burn herself upon the funeral pile of her dead husband, would it be beyond the power of the civil government to prevent her from carrying her belief into practice? So here, as a law for the organization of society under the exclusive dominion of the United States, it is provided that plural marriages shall not be allowed. Can a man excuse his practices to the country because of his religious belief? To permit this would be to make the professed doctrines of religious belief superior to the law of the land, and in effect to permit every citizen to become a law unto himself. Government could exist only in name under such circumstances."

Those words express the views of at least nine tenths of the people in our land. To deny those statements is to deny doctrines that are essential to the possibility of civil government, and in effect would reduce society to a state of anarchy in which every one may do as he pleases without any legal responsibility. Crimes against society do not cease to be crimes because they are religiously committed. Society can never take the criminal's conscience, whether it be religious or otherwise, as a test or guide on this subject, and yet live under the regulation of law. Nevertheless, the Mormons do not agree with us in such views, and hold that every person who is convicted under the Edmunds law is a martyr to his religion.

And looking at the subject as they do, we cannot help but feel a measure of respect for the Mormons while we deplore their bondage, when we find them, after conviction in court, when the alternative is presented to them

of a promise to obey the law against polygamy hereafter
or go to prison, deliberately choose the latter, saying, as
Abram H. Cannon, one of the elders of the Church did,
March 17th, 1886 : " I would like to state, your Honor,
that I have always endeavored to keep the laws of the
United States, because I have been taught by my parents that the Constitution was a sacred instrument. That
I have failed in this respect and now stand before you
convicted of the crime of unlawful cohabitation is due
to the fact that I acknowledge a higher law than that of
man, which is the law of God ; and that law being a
part of my religion, sir, I have attempted to obey it.
When I embraced this religion I promised to place all
that I had, even life itself, upon the altar, and I expect
to abide by that covenant which I made. And, sir, I
hope the day will never come when I must sacrifice
principle even to procure life or liberty. Honor, sir, to
me is higher than anything else upon the earth ; and my
religion is dearer to me than anything else that I have
yet seen. I am prepared, sir, for the judgment of the
court." Such a man one cannot help but respect ; and
we can only wish that he stood up thus manfully in a
nobler cause than that of polygamy.

Shortly after Governor West went to Utah on his
appointment by the President, he visited the penitentiary of the Territory, and in an address to the Mormon
inmates promised them pardon if they would hereafter
obey the law ; but after reflection, the following written
reply was sent to him signed by forty-eight Mormon
prisoners :

"UTAH PENITENTIARY, May 24, 1886.

" *To his Excellency Caleb W. West, Governor of Utah:*

" SIR : On the 13th instant you honored the inmates
of the Penitentiary with a visit and offered to intercede

for the pardon of all those enduring imprisonment on conviction under the Edmunds law, if they would but promise obedience to it in the future, as interpreted by the courts. Gratitude for the interest manifested in our behalf claims from us a reply. We trust, however, that this will not be construed into defiance, as our silence already has been. We have no desire to occupy a defiant attitude toward the Government, or to be in conflict with the nation's laws. We have never been even accused of violating any other law than the one under which we were convicted, and that was enacted purposely to oppose a tenet of our religion.

"We conscientiously believe in the doctrine of plural marriage, and have practised it from a firm conviction of its being a divine requirement.

"Of the forty-nine elders of the Church of Jesus Christ of Latter-Day Saints now imprisoned in the penitentiary for alleged violation of the Edmunds law, all but four had plural wives from its passage to thirty-five years prior to its passage. We were united to our wives for time and eternity by the most sacred covenants, and in many instances numerous children have been born as a result of our union, who are endeared to us by the strongest paternal ties.

"What the promise asked of us implied you declined to explain, just as the courts have done when appeals have been made to them for an explicit and permanent definition of what must be done to comply with the law.

"The rulings of the courts under this law have been too varied and conflicting heretofore for us to know what may be the future interpretations.

"The simple status of plural marriage is now made, under the law, material evidence in securing conviction for unlawful cohabitation, thus, independent of our act, ruthlessly trespassing upon the sacred domain of our religious belief.

"So far as compliance with your proposition requires the sacrifice of honor and manhood, the repudiation of our wives and children, the violation of sacred covenants, Heaven forbid that we should be guilty of such perfidy; perpetual imprisonment, with which we are threatened, or even death itself, would be preferable.

"Our wives desire no separation from us, and were we to comply with your request they would regard our action as most cruel, inhuman, and monstrous, our children would blush with shame, and we should deserve the scorn and contempt of all just and honorable men.

"The proposition you made, though prompted, doubtless, by a kind feeling, was not new, for we could all have avoided imprisonment by making the same promise to the courts; in fact, the penalties we are now enduring are for declining to so promise rather than for acts committed in the past. Had you offered us unconditional amnesty, it would have been gladly accepted; but, dearly as we prize the great boon of liberty, we cannot afford to obtain it by proving untrue to our conscience, our religion, and our God.

"As loyal citizens of this great Republic, whose Constitution we revere, we not only ask for, but claim, our rights as freemen; and if from neither local nor national authority we are to receive equity and mercy, we will make our appeal to the Great Arbiter of all human interests, who in due time will grant us the justice hitherto denied.

"That you may, as the governor of our important but afflicted Territory, aid us in securing every right to which loyal citizens are entitled, and find happiness in so doing, we will ever pray."

Now, this reply is respectful, sincere, and straightforward, yet firm and vigorous, and shows no sign of weakness or indecision. We must credit the signers with the courage of conviction and the qualities which cause men to suffer rather than recant. Such acts show unmistakably the utter futility of law *now* as applied to Mormon polygamy. Had the law which was enacted in 1862 then been rigidly put in force, and, if necessary, supplemented by other legislation to make it effective, Mormon polygamy might ere this have come to an end. Then it was in its first decade of existence, and had not had time to be firmly grounded in the minds of the people as a distinctive article of their faith ; but now it has thirty-five years of open practice back of it, and the example of father and mother, who are stigmatized by any harsh appellation applied to polygamy. Furthermore, the belief in it has been instilled into the minds of the present generation from their childhood, and has become firmly grounded in their belief.

There is one great mistake made by most people in regard to Utah polygamy. They believe that the women of Utah are held by the men in a kind of captivity, not being able to escape from their degradation, but would gladly avail themselves of liberty if they only had an opportunity. The fact is, that they are in voluntary servitude, and would not accept liberty, because *they believe it is their duty to be polygamists.*

There was a mass-meeting of women held in Salt Lake City in the fall of 1878 which was attended by about two thousand women who were devoted Mormons. At that meeting one woman seventy years of age said : " I thank God that I am a polygamous wife ;" and she said she had a " feeling of great pity for those who did not enjoy this good blessing." Another old lady said : " I would not abandon it to exchange with Queen Victoria and all her dependencies." The secretary of the meeting said : "The women of this country want to crush us, but it will be diamond cut diamond." And thus for nearly three hours one speaker after another defended polygamy, all believing it to be an inspired doctrine given by God to aid in redeeming a sinful world from a condition of sin and pollution to one of holiness and purity. The following resolution among others was unanimously adopted by the meeting :

"*Resolved*, That we solemnly avow our belief in the doctrine of the patriarchal order of marriage—a doctrine which was revealed to and practised by God's people in past ages, and is now re-established on earth by divine command of Him who is the same yesterday, to-day, and forever ; a doctrine which, if lived up to and carried out under the direction of the precepts pertaining to it, and of the higher principles of our nature, would conduce to the long life, strength, and glory of the people practising it ; and we therefore indorse it as one of the most important principles of our holy religion, and claim the right of its practice."

It can be plainly seen from that meeting that the leading Mormon women are in earnest in their plea for polygamy, and that it is practised because *they believe God commanded it ;* and consequently it can never be overcome by human law.

SENATOR HOAR, who, with Senator Edmunds, has divided the honor of originating radical laws against Mormon polygamy, seems himself to have acknowledged their worthlessness as an effective remedy. The following letter from him to Joseph Cook was read by the latter in connection with his lecture delivered in Boston, February 2d, 1885 :

"WASHINGTON, January 31, 1885.

"MY DEAR SIR : I am glad that the topics of Mormonism and the reorganization of the South are to be discussed in your lectures in Boston. Massachusetts is an old State. Her people dwell under institutions which have been ripening for two hundred and fifty years; but in the West, in the heart of the Continent, and in the South we are laying foundations still. If Mormonism live and grow, the Christian family will not be an element in the civilization of the great Central States of the future. If the 30,000,000 of the colored race who within fifty years will inhabit the States of the South are to be a race of peasants, denied their practical and equal share in the Government by such processes as have prevailed in recent years, the republic itself cannot continue. The Russian ' despotism tempered by assassination' is quite as desirable as Republicanism tempered by both assassination and fraud. *In the warfare with these things, the school and the Christian Church are to be our most potent instruments. They can accomplish more than any political party.* I have contemplated with the greatest satisfaction the noble work in this cause of our New England churches and of the associations they have organized.

"I am yours, very truly,
"GEORGE F. HOAR."

It is, indeed, true that the school and the Christian Church are more "potent instruments" for the overthrow of polygamy than any laws of our political legislators. Law does not reach the evil, for it rests upon a strong religious conviction. *Law cannot reach it.* To make a law that a man shall not be fanatical is to waste paper on which something sensible might be written; for Congress to undertake to keep people from becoming fanatics is unspeakably ludicrous. Legislation in that direction is intrusive. Law provides for the punishment of an overt act, and is absolutely powerless as to a man's eccentricity.

We do not mean to assert that the laws against polygamy should be stricken from our statute-books. Far from it. On the contrary, it is a shame to our country that they have been allowed so long to be nullified. Let us thank God that during the past two years they have been enforced. They should be most rigidly enforced, although no such system of inquisition and prying into the most sacred relations of husband and wife through their children should be instituted in the name of purity and justice, as the Mormons claim is being now carried on there, and which called forth an earnest protest by the women of Utah at a mass-meeting in the theatre of Salt Lake City March 6th, 1886. Besides, other crimes in the Territory should not be overlooked in zeal to punish that particular crime. The laws should be impartially executed. Moreover, I believe the penalty for the crime should be made to correspond better with the gravity of the crime. Six months' imprisonment seems a very small penalty for such an enormous crime against society ; the Mormons purchase martyrdom at too cheap a price. It should be increased to three or five years' imprisonment.

Nevertheless, no matter what the law may be, it cannot alone overcome this evil. It may make the evil unpopular. It may act upon some as an educator, and cause them to lose their implicit confidence in their leaders ; and, indeed, such is said to be the fact in Utah now. Dr. McNiece, in his letter to the writer from Salt Lake City, dated February 12th, 1886, says : " The people are beginning to lose faith in their leaders.

The Lord is not coming down on the Wahsatch Mountains with horses and chariots of fire to deliver the persecuted (?) Saints, as Orson Pratt used to predict. In fact, the people are beginning to doubt about the Lord's being on their side at all." Now, that is a good sign; and it is, doubtless, true of the more enlightened among the Mormons; but upon the masses of the people, the only effect will be to weld them closer together; and I cannot but think that the leaders are glad that they can raise the cry of persecution. That cry puts down all internal dissension, and unites the people against a common enemy. "The blood of the martyrs is the seed of the Church," has passed into a proverb.

But the plan which we propose has nothing of persecution in connection with it, and thus it will leave room for internal dissension; and from within alone can Mormonism be effectually helped to eradicate its errors. The evils will in this way be overcome by the people themselves, while in reality the work will be accomplished by forces without.

That this system would prove effectual may be safely argued from the fact that, wherever the Gentiles now live in any number, there polygamy is discountenanced and is on the decline. JUDGE C. C. GOODWIN, editor of the Salt Lake *Tribune,* in an article in *Harper's Weekly,* October, 1881, said: "Not half of the daughters of Mormons who have grown up amid a large population of Gentiles will ever enter into polygamy."

Besides, it may be argued from a parallel case, which actually did take place in our own land. The Oneida Community, in the midst of one of the most prosperous and intelligent communities in the State of New York, openly defied popular sentiment and covertly transgressed the law by the maintenance of a social system as abhorrent as that of polygamy; for they practised promiscuous marriage. They were a community having all things in common, and the women were as much common property as any other property. Its members, however, were not mobbed; they were not terrorized in the name of law; they were not driven into exile by persecution; but free contact with the healthful currents of the life about them finally resulted in the disintegration of that portion of their social fabric which was maintained in opposition to law and the sentiment of their neighbors. Now, with that practical example in mind, who would dare say that the scheme we advocate would not be effectual in breaking up polygamy?

Thus we trust that we have shown that this plan would effectually cure the evils of the Mormon social system, and bring the Mormons out of the personal, mental, and moral bondage, which now blinds their eyes and benumbs their sensibilities.

We regard it the duty of the nation to set on foot this peaceful, yet most effective, plan. Let the nation at once establish free schools all over the Territory, to let the rising generation breathe constantly the air of liberty and have the light of knowledge, that the ignorance and superstition which form the cement which keeps the Mormon social system from falling into ruins may not get possession of their minds and souls; and let the nation offer large inducements for colonists to emigrate to Utah, and give them every facility. Money spent in this way is for the general welfare, and is as justifiable as to spend money for a national exposition, or for checking the spread of cholera or yellow-fever. If the nation would do these two things, that accursed system of bondage would disappear within the next decade, and the citizens of Utah would "*be like the rest of us.*"

But if the nation fails to do this, then individual citizens throughout the land, all lovers of humanity, and especially all Christian denominations, should take the matter in hand; and they should not only plant free schools in all parts of the Territory, a few of which have been established already by five different Christian denominations; but they should also form Utah Colonization Societies, whose object should be to secure the planting of pure, freedom-loving, Christian families in every Mormon city, town, and village; and they should not desist until the Mormons are in a minority in Utah, the people freed from their bondage, and the laws respected. Honor demands it; humanity cries out for it; Christianity implores it.

> "Up *now* for Freedom! Not in strife
> Like that your sterner fathers saw—
> The awful waste of human life,
> The glory and the guilt of war;
> But break the chain, the yoke remove,
> And smite to earth Oppression's rod,
> With those mild arms of Truth and Love,
> Made mighty through the Living God!"

PART IV.

THE RELIGIOUS PUZZLE.

"THE true grandeur of nations is in those qualities which constitute the true greatness of the individual."—CHARLES SUMNER.

"A CHRISTIAN is the highest style of man."—YOUNG'S NIGHT THOUGHTS.

"THERE was never law, or sect, or opinion did so magnify goodness as the Christian religion doth."—LORD BACON.

CHAPTER XII.

The religious aspects of Mormonism paramount—General ignorance concerning the Mormon religious system—SOURCES OF THEIR DOCTRINES—Revelation, not reason, the primary source—All religions founded on revelation—Sacred books—The Mormon Bible—The "Book of Mormon"—Migrations of Jews to America—Visit of Jesus to America—"Book of Doctrine and Covenants"—The "Living Oracles."

THE majority of persons are more interested, it seems, in the political and social aspects of the Mormon question than in the purely religious; and this is only natural, because events of a political nature are usually more stirring than any other, and multitudes of people can grow indignant over violations of the law of the land, who at the same time have no deep-seated abhorrence of sin *per se*. The war against polygamy is undoubtedly of great interest to the average citizen; and the Christian himself cannot help sympathizing with the vigorous work of enforcing the law against polygamy, even though he may not always be in sympathy with the spirit of those who make the political phase paramount to every other.

The religious aspects of the question must ever have the pre-eminence in the Christian's mind, because the eternal destinies of thousands of souls are involved in this great heresy, and because Mormonism will continue to have strength and vitality as a religious system, even though it be stripped of its objectionable political and social features. The rank and file of the people are devoted to their creed. They sincerely believe themselves to be the real conservators of the faith once delivered to the Saints, They are fortified by a system of theology as plausible to the darkened understanding as it is pleasing to the natural heart. They are living under a covenant of works, upon which they have staked their all, and they have a hope of abundant rewards in the future. Their conception of the divine law is narrow and inadequate, because their notions respecting God are cramped and carnal. Gross error has become thoroughly rooted in the minds of the people.

As we have already seen in treating of the political and social aspects of Mormonism, *its real power lies in its doctrines.* It is the Mormon's constant boast that nothing can shake the sure foundations of his faith. He has a sincere conviction that his doctrines are invulnerable; but, although the strength of Mormonism does lie in its doctrines, perhaps not one hundredth of the people of our land know anything about their religious tenets, save the doctrine of polygamy.

Let us, therefore, endeavor to get some idea of Mormonism as a religious system—a system of doctrines and precepts; and in doing so let us consider, in the first place,

I. THE SOURCES OF THEIR DOCTRINES.

Mormonism rests not upon human reason as its first great source, but upon divine revelation. It is not a system of *philosophy*, therefore, but a system of *religion;* for Professor Köstlin says: " Without revelation there can be no religion; and it is a fact which should not be overlooked that even those who, on account of their idea of God, absolutely reject the idea of a direct, divine revelation, recognizing nothing but Nature in her material existence and mechanical working, cannot help applying to Nature expressions and conceptions which tend to raise her above the dumb necessity, and constitute her a higher being, capable of moral relations; nor can they for a longer period escape a feeling of thirst after revelations of the secret depths of that being, which they then strive to attain by ways more or less mystical and magical." (Schaff-Herzog's "Encyclopædia of Religious Knowledge," Vol. III., page 2021.) And in accordance with that statement, the editor of the *Independent*, in an editorial note published April 8th, 1886, says : "The history of this world shows that in respect to the subject of religion, the supernatural is to human thought and feeling really the natural. We search that history in vain for a religious system that has stamped itself upon the faith and practice of men, operating upon them as a controlling power of comfort and hope, and organizing itself into their personal and social life by forms, usages, and modes of worship, and at the same time professedly based on the discoveries and authority of unaided human reason. Philosophies in abundance have been the products of such reason, but religious systems never. All the idolatries of antiquity claimed to be supernatural, and the same is true of all the forms of modern heathenism. Such is the assumed character of Mohammedanism and Mormonism. . . . The world never has had, and, judging by the past, never will have a religious system without this element. It does not want, and will not accept, a religion that claims for itself no higher basis than that of mere reason."

"*Thus saith the Lord*" is the one claim of all the religious systems of the world. Accordingly we find that the adherents of all the great religions have their sacred books, which they venerate as revelations from heaven, from whence they claim their doctrines have emanated. The Brahmin has his Vedas ; the Buddhist has his Tripitaka; the Zoroastrian has his Avesta; the Jew has the Law and the Prophets; the Christian has the Old and New Testaments; the Mohammedan has the Koran. In like manner, the Mormon has the "*Book of Mormon.*" But the Book of Mormon is not the only inspired book of the Latter-Day Saints. They adopt the Bible, the "Book of Mormon," and the "Book of Doctrine and Covenants," as their inspired Scriptures; and these are the sources of their doctrines.

1. *The Mormon Bible.*—By those not familiar with Mormon literature, the Mormon Bible and the "Book of Mormon" are frequently confounded. The former, however, is simply our English version of the Scriptures, with such modifications and distortions as Joseph Smith, the inspired translator, saw fit to make. He twisted some passages in Genesis so as to turn statements connected with the life of the patriarch Joseph into prophecies relating to a great prophet called Joseph, who should come forth in the latter days—referring to himself. He even had the audacity to make interpolations in Christ's Sermon on the Mount; but our Bible, as translated by Smith and interpreted by him and his successors, is accepted by every Mormon as inspired, and is to be found in every Mormon Church.

2. *The "Book of Mormon"* is the next source of their doctrines, and is the more modern revelation, and therefore takes precedence over the Bible. The supernatural origin of the book, according to the Mormon belief, we have already given in Chapter I.

Mormon, after whom the book is called, was the last of the sacred prophets of ancient America. He was the leader of a race called the Nephites, and perished in a battle between his own race and the Lamanites in A.D. 420.

Both Nephites and Lamanites were descendants from the family of Lehi, an Israelite of the tribe of Manasseh, who emigrated from Jerusalem to America during the reign of King Zedekiah, 600 B.C.

The wars between these two races form the great bulk of the book. In the year A.D. 420 the decisive battle was fought at Cummorah, in Western New York. The Nephites were exterminated, with the exception of a few individuals. Mormon, their leader, was slain, and with him 230,000. The descendants of the victorious Lamanites are the North American Indians.

The "Book of Mormon" is said to be the condensed record of the history, faith, and prophecies of the ancient inhabitants of America, made on golden plates by the prophet Mormon. These plates he intrusted to his son Moroni, who survived the awful battle of extermination. He was the last of the Nephites to die, but before dying he sealed up the golden plates on which all these events were written and hid them in the Hill Cummorah, the very site of the final battle between the Nephites and Lamanites; and there Joseph Smith, guided by the spirit of Moroni himself, found them in 1827, took them to his home, translated them by means of his magical spectacles, and had them printed under the title " *The Book of Mormon.*"

It is certainly a unique work. It is a collection of sixteen separate or distinct books professing to be written at different periods by different prophets. Its style is in imitation of the Bible, and it incorporates about three hundred passages directly from the Holy Scriptures.

Among the records of the book are accounts of three different migrations to the American Continent: 1. A colony from the Tower of Babel soon after the flood, which was led by Jared, and which in time became a great nation, but was destroyed for their sins. 2. A colony led by Lehi from Jerusalem, which gave rise to the Nephites and Lamanites. 3. A number of Israelites who came from Jerusalem about eleven years after Lehi.

The book also declares that a supernatural light which lasted three days and three nights informed the inhabitants of America of the birth of Christ, and later a terrible earthquake announced His crucifixion; and three days afterward Jesus Himself appeared, descending out of heaven into the chief city of the Nephites in the sight of the people, to whom He exhibited His wounded side and the prints of the nails in His hands and feet. He remained with them forty days, and repeated to them His Sermon on the Mount, and appointed twelve American apostles, and gave them orders regarding baptism and His holy communion.

This book was the foundation of Mormonism; and Sidney Rigdon said: "The 'Book of Mormon' is to govern the Millennial Church;" but whatever may have been its uses to the Saints in the beginning of their career, it has had little to do with their practices for many years, save as a text-book.

3. *The " Book of Doctrine and Covenants."*—Another source of Mormon doctrine—and a more fruitful source than the Book of Mormon—is the " Book of Doctrine and Covenants." This is a collection of all the multifarious revelations that Joseph Smith claimed to receive and which he promulgated, together with the only revelation put forth by Brigham Young—the one which he set forth at Council Bluffs in 1847 to inspire and guide the Saints in their projected western pilgrimage through the wilderness.

4. *Living Oracles.*—The fourth source of Mormon doctrine is what has well been called the "Living

Oracles," the divine communications made continually to the priesthood. Theoretically the Mormons hold the Bible and their two sacred books to be the inspired Scriptures for their guidance : the Old Testament, as addressed particularly to the Jewish Church ; the New Testament to the Judaic and European Christian Church ; the "Book of Mormon" to the Church of America, and the "Book of Doctrine and Covenants" to the Church of Jesus Christ of Latter-Day Saints. But practically, authority and guidance for them emanate from their living leaders, and few of either chiefs or masses read any of the three sacred books in order to know and follow the recorded teachings.

Thus Mormonism, through its belief in a continual revelation to the priesthood, especially the First Presidency and the Twelve Apostles, has marvellous ability to change itself to meet every emergency.

CHAPTER XIII.

THE RELIGIOUS PUZZLE (*continued*).

MORMON DOCTRINES—Their idea of God—Plurality of gods—Mormon Sunday-school hymn concerning Smith—The pre-existence of souls—The doctrine of Polygamy—Practised on the plea of self-sacrifice and ambition—Necessity of preaching their gospel to all—Preaching to the dead—Baptismal regeneration—Baptism for the dead—Mormon priesthood necessary to salvation—Melchizedek and Aaronic priesthoods—Mormon Endowments—Blood Atonement—Doctrine of "The Fulness of Times."

HAVING thus considered the sources of Mormon doctrine—the ways in which God has revealed His will and purposes unto them—let us consider in the second place some of their

II. DOCTRINES AND PRACTICES.

1. *Their idea of God is materialistic.* While they profess to believe the Trinity, they say that God was once a man, who has advanced in intelligence and power so much that now He may be called perfect; but He has still the form and figure of a man.

One of the standard Mormon works is called a "Key to the Science of Theology," written by Parley P. Pratt, who, while he lived, was one of the Twelve Apostles. It is now used as a text-book among the people. In confirmation of the statement that they hold grossly corporeal ideas concerning God, it says: "God has an organized individual tabernacle embodied in material form and composed of material substance, in the likeness of man, and possessing every organ, limb, and physical part that man possesses."

Christ, too, is believed to have been the offspring of the material union on the plains of Palestine of God and the Virgin Mary. Yet Christ is believed to have had a previous existence, and His worship is enjoined as Lord of all. The Holy Ghost, or Paraclete, is also material. Thus do they lower the divinity to humanity instead of lifting up humanity to the divinity.

2. Another doctrine is that of *Plurality of gods.*

Though there is one God supreme, there are many other beings entitled to the name because possessed of the attributes of God, such as creative power. All these gods were once men, and all men are potential gods. The book of Parley Pratt, already quoted, says : " It will be recollected that the last chapter recognizes a family of gods, or, in other words, a species of beings who have physical tabernacles of flesh and bones in the form of man, but so constructed as to be capable of eternal life. . . . A general assembly, quorum, or grand council of the gods, with their president at their head, constitute the designing and creating power. . . . Wisdom inspires the gods to multiply their species and to lay the foundation for all the forms of life to increase in numbers, and for each to enjoy himself in the sphere to which he is adapted."

Adam is said to be the god of Jesus Christ, Jesus Christ the god of Joseph Smith, and Joseph Smith the god of this generation. They teach their children that Joseph Smith is their god, and their little ones hear more of him than they do of Jesus. Even in their hymns is this great error taught. I will give one of the hymns found in their "Primary Hymn-Book," which is sung by the children in the Mormon Sunday-schools, called by them "Primary Associations." It is as follows:

"The seer, the seer, Joseph the seer!
I'll sing of the Prophet ever dear;
His equal now cannot be found
By searching the wide world around.
With gods he soared in the realms of day,
And men he taught the heavenly way.
The earthly Sun, the Heavenly Sun!
I love to dwell on his memory dear;
The chosen of God and the friend of man—
He brought the Priesthood back again;
He gazed on the past; on the present, too,
And opened the heavenly world to view.

"Of noble seed, of heavenly birth,
He came to bless the sons of earth.
With keys by the Almighty given
He opened the full rich stores of heaven.
O'er the world that was wrapt in sable night,
Like the sun he spread his golden light.
He strove, oh, how he strove to stay
The stream of crime in its reckless way;
With a mighty mind and a noble aim,
He urged the wayward to reclaim;
'Mid the foaming billows of angry strife
He stood at the helm of the ship of life.
The Saints, the Saints, his only pride!
For them he lived, for them he died.
Their joys were his—their sorrows, too;
He loved the Saints and he loved Nauvoo.
Unchanged by death, with a Saviour's love
He pleads their cause in the courts above.
The seer, the seer, Joseph the seer!
Oh, how I love his memory dear!
The just and wise, the pure and free,
A father he was and is to me.
Let friends now rage in their dark hour,
No matter—he is beyond their power.

"He's free! He's free! the Prophet's free!
He is where he will ever be

> Beyond the reach of mobs and strife.
> He rests unharmed, in endless life ;
> His home's in the sky, he dwells with the gods,
> Far from the furious rage of mobs.
> He died, he died for those he loved—
> He reigns, he reigns in the realms above !
> He waits with the just who have gone before
> To welcome the saints to Zion's shore.
> Shout, shout, ye Saints ! this boon is given—
> We'll meet our martyred seer in heaven."

Thus are the Mormon children early taught to think of Joseph Smith as their Saviour, and as divine. Brigham Young, too, was regarded as God by some of his followers even before his death ; and no doubt before long, when they forget to some extent his misdeeds that have been brought to light since his death, they will deify him as well as Joseph Smith. Indeed, they teach that all Mormons may, by obedience and holiness, become gods in the celestial world, and people and rule a kingdom forever. Helped by polygamy, men may become makers of worlds like this, of which Adam was the fashioner ; and in those worlds their posterity become the creatures over whom they bear sway.

3. Another doctrine is *The Pre-existence of Souls.*

All men lived before they were born. They existed for ages as spirits, waiting eagerly for fleshly tabernacles ; and multitudes of these spirits are now waiting, desiring to come to earth ; for it is only by the way of the flesh that they can reach the final bliss of their perfected being, and therefore it is a work of great benevolence to provide earthly bodies into which they may come to dwell.

4. *The Doctrine of Polygamy* springs naturally out of the two preceding doctrines. In the " Book of Mormon" this practice was forbidden ; and in the earlier revela-

tions of Joseph Smith it was distinctly condemned; but it was sanctioned in a revelation claimed to have been given to him at Nauvoo, July 12th, 1843, although it was not promulgated until the fall of 1852 in Salt Lake City by Brigham Young. This doctrine is a necessary sequence of their ideas with regard to the celestial world and the pre-existent life of the human soul. Mr. Pratt, in one of his sermons, says : " The spirit that dwells in each man and woman is, I venture to say, more than five thousand years old. The Lord has ordained that these spirits should come here and take tabernacles by a certain law and through a certain channel; and *that* law is the law of marriage. The Lord ordained marriage on this globe between Adam and Eve as eternal in its nature ; hence we believe in marrying for eternity. Among these spirits in the heavens are many more noble, more intelligent, that were called the great and mighty ones, who were reserved till the fulness of time to come forth upon the face of the earth through a noble parentage, who shall train their tender minds in the truths of eternity, that they may be prophets, priests, and kings to the Most High God. Among the Saints is the most likely place for these spirits to take their tabernacles, to be trained up by that people that are the most righteous of any other people upon the earth. This is the reason that the Lord is sending them here, brethren and sisters. The Lord has not kept them in reserve for five or six thousand years, waiting for their bodies, to send them to the Hottentots, the Hindoos, or the negroes, but to the Saints of Zion. Then, is it not reasonable that the Lord should say unto his faithful and chosen servants : ' Take unto yourselves more wives, that more of these noble spirits should come forth through these my faithful and chosen servants ' ?"

Thus do the Mormons have as one of the underlying principles of this abominable practice one of the grandest sentiments of humanity—*self-sacrifice for the sake of others*. It is that sentiment which has taken hold of the Mormon women and led them not only to submit in silence to what is entirely counter to their nature, but even to choose it and glory in it. Brigham Young told his people often that the world was rapidly hastening to a close, and there were multitudes of spirits waiting for honorable bodies. The Gentiles were corrupt, and the ethereal spirits were waiting anxiously for the favors of the Mormons. The women, he said, would be selfish if they could not endure the wandering affections of their husbands. It was their duty to make a self-sacrifice. Jesus had given His life to redeem; why could they not help to save? It is on that account that *the women of Utah* have made the sacrifice of the most vital principle of their souls.

The principle which has led *the Mormon men* to embrace this doctrine, which greatly increases their earthly cares and burdens, is *ambition*. In heaven they will rule over their posterity; and, consequently, the more wives they have, and the greater their posterity, the greater will be their rank in heaven. Orson Hyde, in one of his sermons, said: "The revelation of the Almighty to a man . . . whom God designs to make a ruler and a governor in his eternal kingdom is that he may have more wives, that when he goes to another sphere he may still continue to perpetuate his species; and of his kingdom there shall be no end.". The Mormons declare that those who have no wives are the servants of those who rule. Therefore the object of the Mormon men in embracing polygamy, as they themselves set forth, is to raise up a numerous posterity here and in the world to come, that they may be exalted to the rank of "gods to reign upon thrones." They believe that all the gods have many wives, and they rule over their descendants, who are constantly increasing in number and dominion; and in accordance with that belief, they teach that Jesus was a polygamist, and that Mary and Martha were his plural wives, with whom he is now living in marriage relations in the celestial world.

5. Another doctrine is that *the Latter-Day Gospel must be preached to all men.* Until that gospel is accepted, none can be saved; and so, from the earliest days, zeal for propagandism has been a marked feature of this sect. At the very soonest the world must be conquered by this gospel. This has from the first been their fixed design, and about three hundred missionaries are always in the field. The order is: first, offer salvation to the Gentiles till the Lord proclaims that their opportunity is past, and then turn to the Jews. Moreover, they believe there is need for hot haste; for these are the latter days, and the dread second coming of the Son of God is at hand. Many of the devout Mormons believe that when the great temple in Salt Lake City is finished, the Lord Jesus will descend to earth and reign with His Saints for a thousand years.

But not only can none be saved until the Mormon gospel is accepted; neither can any be condemned till it has been heard and rejected by him. And so, not only must *the living* hear the Latter-Day Gospel, but the same proclamation must be made through all the bounds of the great gathering-place of the dead. To these "spirits in prison," whose sad misfortune it was to die before the Hill of Cummorah gave up its golden plates to the great Prophet, must be made the offer of faith and baptism. Hence, when Mormon missionaries die they go on preaching just as before—so great is the task, so distant the goal, set before this peculiar people.

6. They also believe in *Baptismal Regeneration.* They bless little children, but baptize none under the age of eight. They practice the mode of immersion, and they teach that it is able to wash away sins, and that it may be repeated for the remission of sins whenever it is needed. Consequently, when any of the Saints fall into heinous sins, they are taught that those sins can be washed away by their being rebaptized.

7. They also believe in *Baptism for the Dead.* They base this doctrine on Paul's statement in the fifteenth chapter of the First Epistle to the Corinthians. They claim that since three things are essential to salvation—faith, repentance, and baptism—and the latter is not possible in the world of spirits, one in order to be saved after death must be baptized by proxy—*i.e.*, some Saint on earth must be immersed in his behalf. It is claimed that here Mormonism is most unique, and performs its noblest service to the race. In this way the Mormons save their ancestors from everlasting punishment, and bring their souls within Zion; and this service is extended beyond relatives, too, and is given to the heroes and heroines of history. Washington, Franklin, and other famous men have thus been vicariously baptized into the Mormon Church. A writer on Mormonism has well said : " In fact, no one is safe from the clutches of Mormonism after death. You may be made a Mormon without desiring it for all eternity."

It is said that in the summer of 1884 a wealthy Mormon, while on a visit to Boston, employed a young lady to look up his genealogy. Having learned the names of about two hundred of his ancestors, he had the rite of baptism performed for them all. And it is related that an old man, long a convert to Mormonism, residing in the southern part of Utah, went thirty miles distant to a place where the Saints were in conference for the purpose of saving nearly one hundred of his ancestors from everlasting destruction by being baptized for them. He made the journey in an ox-cart with his two sons. The baptism, of course, was immersion in a river; and the old man was dipped as many times as he could stand the operation, each dip representing an entrance into the Mormon paradise for some one of the otherwise lost hundred of his forefathers; and then his sons in turn were baptized, until the object of their visit was fully accomplished.

8. Another doctrine is that *a priesthood duly authorized by God is absolutely essential to salvation.* Without this no sacrament or rite is acceptable to God or of value to men. It is only through their preaching that sinners can repent and believe; and the remission of sins follows baptism only when priestly hands administer it; and this authority comes by no fancied apostolical succession, but from Joseph Smith as the sole source. Before him for a thousand years there was no authority, and to-day all is illegitimate outside the Mormon Church.

There are two classes of priesthood: *The Melchizedek* and *the Aaronic.* The Melchizedek priesthood is the higher branch, having special reference to spiritual affairs, while the Aaronic priesthood has most to do with the temporal interests of the Church. Both of these branches are obtained through Joseph Smith, who received his ordination in a supernatural manner. According to Mormon authority, an angelic messenger, calling himself John the Baptist, met him in the woods of New York, May 15th, 1829, and ordained him to the

Aaronic priesthood; and soon after, it is claimed, he received his ordination to the Melchizedek priesthood at the hands of the apostles Peter, James, and John.

The Aaronic priesthood includes (beginning with the lowest) the offices of deacon, teacher, priest, and bishop. The Melchizedek priesthood includes the offices of elder, high-priest, patriarch, seventy, and apostle. A worse despotism than is exercised over the people by this priesthood cannot be found on earth. Claiming to have the keys of heaven and hell, and to have its authority directly from the Lord, it wields absolute power, not only in spiritual but in all temporal affairs.

9. Another peculiar doctrine is with reference to *Endowments*. To get one's endowments constitutes one of the most exalted privileges and ambitions of the devout Mormon. These can be had only in Utah and in connection with the temples, although in Salt Lake City, where as yet the temple is unfinished, the Endowment House is used. After divers washings and anointings and rubbings, the acting of an historic drama, the taking of oaths and grips, and the giving of a new name, celestial wisdom and joy are supposed to descend and forever rest upon the favored soul. Secret marriage rites, which seal husband and wife for time and eternity, form part of the ceremony.

In that hour, also, is put on the "endowment robe," a garment reaching from head to foot, and made all in one piece, high-necked and with long sleeves. This robe is said to be a sure defence against the adversary and all physical ills. One must never be caught without it; but if, living and dying, he wears that garment, and remembers the grips and his celestial name, he is sure of heaven whatever may befall him.

The rites of the Endowment House are said to be a

kind of bastard Masonry, instituted by Joseph Smith at Nauvoo. A remarkable resemblance has been pointed out between the ancient Eleusinian Mysteries and the mysteries of the Endowment House as they are represented by some of the historians of Mormonism. Their object, according to Brigham Young, is "to receive all those ordinances in the house of the Lord which are necessary for you, after you have departed this life, to enable you to walk back to the presence of the Father, passing the angels, who stand as sentinels, being enabled to give them the key-words, the signs and tokens pertaining to the holy priesthood, and gain your eternal exaltation in spite of earth and hell."

10. Another doctrine, which is peculiarly a Mormon doctrine, and the most horrible doctrine ever taught by their leaders, is the doctrine of *Blood Atonement*.

According to this doctrine there are some sins which cannot be forgiven or atoned for except by cutting the throat of the man who committed them and pouring out his blood as an atonement. Three of these sins are apostasy, disclosing the secrets of the Endowment House, and marital unfaithfulness on the part of a wife.

This doctrine has been frequently taught by the leaders of the Church, who have declared that it is a meritorious act for any Saint to spill the blood of a person guilty of any of these sins, and that he would thereby be carrying out the golden rule of love. Thus, Brigham Young, in a sermon delivered in the Bowery at Salt Lake City, September 21st, 1856, said : "There are sins that men commit for which they cannot receive forgiveness in this world or in that which is to come, and if they had their eyes open to see their true condition they would be perfectly willing to have their blood spilled upon the ground, that the smoke thereof might ascend to heaven as an offering for their sins ; and the smoking incense would atone for their sins, whereas, if such is not the case, they will stick to them and remain upon them in the spirit world.

"I know when you hear my brethren telling about cutting people off from the earth that you consider it strong doctrine ; but it is to save them, not to destroy them."

And in another discourse, delivered in the Tabernacle of Salt Lake City, February 8th, 1857, Brigham Young said : "I have known a great many men who have left this Church, for whom there is no chance whatever for exaltation ; but if their blood had been spilled, it would have been better for them. This is loving our neighbor as ourselves ; if he needs help, help him ; and if he wants salvation, and it is necessary to spill his blood on the earth in order that he may be saved, spill it. Any of you who understand the principles of eternity, if you have sinned a sin requiring the shedding of blood, except the sin unto death, would not be satisfied nor rest until your blood should be spilled, that you might gain that salvation you desire. This is the way to love mankind."

But although this horrible doctrine has been publicly preached again and again, yet many of the Mormons deny that it was ever carried into actual practice. The editor of the *Deseret News*, one of the Mormon leaders, not long ago denied that blood atonement had ever been practised among the Mormons, but he said "in the good time coming it will be." On the other hand, it is claimed by many Gentiles that not only has it been put into practice frequently in past years, but that it is actually done at the present time. A Gentile observer, after several months' residence in Salt Lake City in 1884, wrote : "As to the blood atonement, which Mormons generally deny, you may be sure it is still practised."

After a careful study of the facts in the case, it seems to be clear that the evidence is overwhelming in substantiation of the declaration that *it was often practised in the past;* and it seems to be equally clear that, while it *may* be *the fact* that this abominable practice is still carried on, only more adroitly than formerly, yet *the mass of evidence* is overwhelming in opposition to that view and in favor of the opinion that the incoming of thousands of Gentiles and Federal officers have effectually stopped the practice of that barbarous doctrine. *Nevertheless, it remains one of their doctrines.*

11. Another Mormon doctrine, and one of which much is made, is the doctrine of the *Fulness of Times.* The Mormons claim that whatever good thing in doctrine and practice has ever existed in the world under former dispensations has been restored in these last days ; and so to the Latter-Day Saints have come all the blessings of all past ages, especially the priesthood, polygamy, and all the offices and gifts of the days of the apostles. They believe the day of miracles has not ceased, but that many such have been wrought, especially healings of the sick, in the latter-day dispensation. They believe, also, in giving one tenth of their income and increase for the building of the temples and the progress of the Church.

CHAPTER XIV.

THE RELIGIOUS PUZZLE (*continued*).

Professor Coyner's analysis of Mormonism—*Rev. Dr. McNiece's* analysis—Reasons for the growth and tenacity of Mormonism—The Christian element its chief source of strength—No Mormon converts from heathenism—Protestantism the source of its recruits—Bible doctrines in the Mormon "Catechism for Children"—The Mormon Articles of Faith—The Mormon heresy compared with Gnosticism in the early Christian Church—A clue to the solution of the religious puzzle.

FROM the enumeration of some of the prominent and peculiar doctrines of Mormonism which was given in the preceding chapter, it can very clearly be seen that it is naught else than a jumble of a half dozen different systems of religion.

Professor Coyner, Principal of the Salt Lake Collegiate Institute for ten years, has analyzed it as follows: "Mormonism is made of twenty parts. Take eight parts of diabolism, three parts of animalism from the Mohammedan system, one part bigotry from old Judaism, four parts cunning and treachery from Jesuitism, two parts Thugism from India, and two parts Arnoldism, and then shake the mixture over the fires of animal passion and throw in the forms and ceremonies of the Christian religion, and you will have this system in its true component elements." But, subtle as that analysis is, it cannot be true; for it does not include in the system, as even one of its twenty parts, Christianity; and yet it seems to me that it is the Christian element in the system which, mingled with a great deal of error, gives it its real strength.

The analysis given by *Rev. Dr. R. G. McNiece*, of Salt Lake City, in the *Presbyterian Review*, April, 1881, seems to be more correct, and about as near the real truth as any one, perhaps, can come. He says: "Let Paganism, Judaism, Mohammedanism, Jesuitism, Protestantism, and Diabolism be shaken up together, and the result is Mormonism; for from Paganism comes its idea of God; from Judaism its theory of the priesthood and special revelation; from Mohammedanism its plural wife notions, and its sensual ideas of heaven; from Jesuitism its cunning and arbitrary form of government, in which the end is continually made to justify the means; from Protestantism its talk about faith in Christ and the guidance of the Holy Spirit; and its general policy from the devil, as any intelligent man will have to confess after a careful study of its cunning, devilish ways and means." From this analysis it is seen that its great strength lies in the shrewd way in which it has blended Christian truth with heathen error.

The reasons of its growth and tenacity are many. It is especially adapted to the intellectual capacities of the masses. To these are offered just what they are sure to hunger after—bold assumption and boundless assertion, together with great show of authority. For the superstitious it has miracles, ecstasies, visions, and revelations. The secrecy of the endowments, too, has a charm. The minds of the ignorant delight in prodigies. "*Omne ignotum, pro mirifico.*" For the lovers of prophecy there is promised the New Jerusalem, an actual reign of the Saints, and an equality with the Redeemer. The gross see charms in its sensual paradise, and listen eagerly to the announcement that a conversation with their spiritual ruler, or a journey on a mission while facing a frowning world, will immediately clear them from their iniquities. These are all elements in the system, which have led to its growth, and now keep it from falling to pieces.

But *its chief source of strength is its recognition of many of the truths of the Bible.* If its strength came from its heathenish doctrines and practices, then it would naturally follow that its converts would be gathered mainly from heathendom, whereas ninety-nine proselytes in every hundred have been obtained from Christian churches.

About thirty years ago swarms of Mormon missionaries were sent to China, Japan, India, Australia, South Africa, South America, and the Society and Sandwich Islands, and they fondly hoped that many converts would be gathered; but in less than five years they had all returned, completely baffled and disgusted. They reported that the devil was far too lively in those lands, and that, among the Hindoos especially, stupidity and awful depravity were universal. Since then we hear of no more attempts to evangelize the pagan world. A few hundred Sandwich Islanders and New Zealanders have been baptized, but only after American and English missionaries had first brought them to a knowledge of Gospel truth.

And it is said that no Roman Catholic has ever been brought into the Mormon fold, Protestantism furnishing Mormonism its entire supplies. Yes, the fact is that Mormonism has grown in strength and power by the addition of those once members of Protestant Christian churches, or those very near the entrance. Perhaps eight out of every ten who have come to Utah were of that class; and it cannot well be questioned that hundreds of so-called Mormons, though laboring under a great delusion and greatly misled by the hierarchy, are still sincere believers in Christ and His Gospel. Rev. Dr. McNiece says in the *Presbyterian Review*, April, 1881 : " It is only just to say that scattered all through the Mormon ranks are hundreds of devout, worthy, kind-hearted, hospitable people, who came from England, Scotland, and the Scandinavian countries, bringing their Bibles and Christian sentiments with them, and who, although nominally Mormons, have never been persuaded to embrace these odious pagan doctrines, which are the distinctive features of Mormonism."

Besides, the Mormons believe in the Old and New Testaments as inspired, and in the "Book of Mormon" itself there is much that is taken directly from the Bible —as the Decalogue, the Sermon on the Mount, and other teachings of our Lord ; and in their "Catechism for Children," published in 1877, one finds mingled with many false teachings such sound biblical propositions as these : that our first parents, having fallen under the influence of Satan, "had not the least power to recover themselves from the effects of that fall ;" that in this condition "the justice of God required a sacrifice to atone for the broken law, and our first parents being subject, through transgression, to the penalty of the law, could not make this sacrifice ;" that to meet such a state of things, "God sent His only begotten Son, who knew no sin, to die for the sins of the world, and thus to satisfy divine justice ;" that "this redemption by Jesus Christ is the only one," and that it is available to all mankind, "but only on conditions of obedience ;" that these conditions are "as unchangeable as their Author," and include faith, which is described as "a principle of power" within the soul, and repentance, which is defined as a "forsaking of sin, with full purpose of heart to work righteousness;" and that even little children are "considered sinners in the sight of God," and as such are "redeemed solely through the atonement of Christ," and are therefore to be taught to repent and believe.

In reading such statements, and seeing them corroborated continually by quotations from Scripture, it is not hard to imagine ourselves studying the catechism of some Christian sect, differing from other sects in detail and expression, but agreeing with them in the essentials of the common Christianity. How far such truths are proclaimed by the Mormon teachers and missionaries, or how far they still remain as vital convictions in the breasts of thousands who once professed them in other communions, or who have been taught them catechetically in the Mormon fold, it is very difficult to determine.

In the Mormon Articles of Faith there is very little but what could be subscribed to by some Christian denomination. It is presumed that these Articles comprise all the essential beliefs of Mormonism. They are what their missionaries constantly teach, and what the Mormons always give forth as their creed. They are just one third the number of the Thirty-nine Articles of the Church of England. They are as follows:

"1. We believe in God, the Eternal Father, and in His Son, Jesus Christ, and in the Holy Ghost.

"2. We believe that men will be punished for their own sins, and not for Adam's transgression.

"3. We believe that, through the atonement of Christ, all mankind may be saved, by obedience to the laws and ordinances of the Gospel.

"4. We believe that these ordinances are: First, faith in the Lord Jesus Christ; second, repentance; third, baptism by immersion for the remission of sins;

fourth, laying on of hands for the gift of the Holy Ghost.

"5. We believe that a man must be called of God by 'prophecy and by the laying on of hands' by those who are in authority to preach the Gospel and administer the ordinances thereof.

"6. We believe in the same organization that exists in the Primitive Church—viz.: apostles, prophets, teachers, evangelists, etc.

"7. We believe in the gift of tongues, prophecy, revelation, visions, healing, interpretation of tongues, etc.

"8. We believe the Bible to be the Word of God, as far as it is translated correctly; we also believe the 'Book of Mormon' to be the Word of God.

"9. We believe all that God has revealed, all that He does now reveal, and we believe that He will yet reveal many great and important things pertaining to the kingdom of God.

"10. We believe in the literal gathering of Israel, and in the restoration of the Ten Tribes; that Zion will be built upon this continent; that Christ will reign personally upon this earth, and that the earth will be renewed and receive its paradisic glory.

"11. We claim the privilege of worshipping Almighty God according to the dictates of our conscience, and allow all men the same privilege; let them worship how, when, or where they will.

"12. We believe in being subject to kings, presidents, rulers, and magistrates; in obeying, honoring, and sustaining the law.

"13. We believe in being honest, true, chaste, benevolent, virtuous, and in doing good to all men; indeed, we say that we follow the admonition of Paul: 'We believe all things; we hope all things;' we have endured many things, and hope to endure all things. If there is anything virtuous, lovely, or of good report, or praiseworthy, we seek after these things."

The fact is, that this nineteenth century heresy bears much the same relation to the Gospel of to-day that Gnosticism, Montanism, and Manicheism did to that of the early centuries. On the true foundation of the Old and New Testaments, it has built a structure of wood, hay, and stubble. "To the law and the testimony," is the constant cry. Argument is based almost entirely upon the Bible. Proof-texts are quoted by the thousand.

Our object in directing attention to the Christian element in Mormonism is not to furnish apology or to divert attention from its fearful errors; but it is mentioned because it furnishes a decided clue to the vitality and persistency of the system, and also opens our eyes as to the best way to solve the religious puzzle which this system presents before us. The great question to be answered is: How are we to get rid of *the erroneous doctrines of Mormonism?*

CHAPTER XV.

THE RELIGIOUS PUZZLE (*concluded*).

The character of efforts hitherto put forth to solve the puzzle—What has been accomplished—The plan somewhere defective—Mormonism to be reformed, not destroyed—Why Mormons will not listen to Christian missionaries—Moody and Sankey's meetings in Salt Lake City—*The Deseret Evening News* on Bishop Tuttle's sermon—Mormonism a perversion of Christianity—The educational and colonization scheme best fitted to reform it—Proved by comparing Roman Catholicism in the United States with Roman Catholicism in Mexico or Brazil—The probable effect of a larger intelligence—The probable effect of the introduction of Gentile colonies—The religious puzzle solved—The duty of the hour.

HITHERTO the efforts which have been put forth against Mormonism as a religious system have been the same in character as when contending with Buddhism, Confucianism, or any other pagan religion. *And what has been accomplished ?*

It is not our desire to depreciate what has been done in Utah by the noble Christian men and women who have faced the insults of men and sometimes death itself in battling with the errors of Mormonism. They are Christian heroes and heroines, and are deserving of all praise and honor. They are worthy to receive crowns and laurels that can never fade. But their sterling worth and Christian heroism do not alter the facts concerning the visible results of their labors. It is true that nearly twenty years elapsed after the occupation of Salt Lake Valley by the Mormons before any attempt was made to introduce the Gospel. It was only by the occupation of Camp Douglas, in 1862, by several regiments of United States troops that the way began to be opened; and only since 1865 has there been any missionary work done in the Territory. But in the twenty years of missionary work what has been accomplished? How many converts from Mormonism have been obtained?

Rev. R. G. McNiece, D.D., of Salt Lake City, in a personal letter to the writer, said: "The number of converts directly from the Mormon ranks I cannot give you; but it is very small, especially among adults. Among the youth the number is greater, and here is where the hope lies. The children and youth come under Christian influence first in the day-schools maintained by the Christian denominations. In the Sabbath-school this influence is deepened, and thereby the way into the Church is opened. I should say that THREE HUNDRED WOULD BE A LARGE ESTIMATE OF THE TOTAL NUMBER OF CHRISTIAN CONVERTS FROM THE MORMON RANKS; but the work thus far has been preparatory."

Now, while it is very true that the work has been in great measure preparatory, nevertheless no such long preparation as twenty years should be necessary in dealing with a people to a great extent speaking our own language. If it were China, or Japan, or India just opened, and it required time for the missionaries to get acquainted with the habits and language of the people, it would be a very different thing. It seems from the small crop of Christian converts thus far obtained that the system of missionary work adopted is somewhere defective.

And does not the fact of the large Christian element in the Mormon religious system show that it must not be treated as a pagan religion? and that different methods must be adopted to overcome its evils? All missionary labor in Utah up to the present time has been in open and direct antagonism to the whole Mormon system, and its object has been openly and professedly to exterminate it from the face of the earth. Now, we raise the question, *Can any Christian sect be easily annihilated?* Should it be our desire to exterminate it? Should not the object of all our efforts be *to reform it*—to purge the gold of its dross? And so, does it not seem far more likely that Mormonism is not to be *destroyed* at all, but rather *reformed* by various influences brought to bear upon it?

The adult Mormons will not go to hear the Christian missionaries, for they believe that all that is good in Christianity they have already in their own system. The only difference is that they have more; they have an enlarged and expanded Christianity. Consequently they think their system is vastly superior to the Christian's. Mormon boys write "*Come to Jesus*" on the clean, white window-sills of Christian chapels, while their parents at home tell them that they know a hundredfold more truth than the Christians, whose whole creed, they say, begins and ends with this despised phrase.

The evangelists Moody and Sankey held a series of meetings in Salt Lake City only a few years ago, and the *Deseret Evening News*, the official Mormon organ, in an editorial on Moody's preaching in that city, said: "There is not a man among the whole fraternity of evangelists who can present anything of any value to the Latter-Day Saints which they have not already received; and there is no preacher of them all who, if he were desirous of learning the truth as it is in Jesus, but could learn very many valuable lessons in the things of God from members of our Young People's Improvement Associations, and even from our Sunday-school children. 'Believe in the Lord Jesus Christ' is a saying the full meaning of which is appreciated by the Latter-Day Saints. To exhort them to 'faith in Christ' is the work of supererogation."

And shortly after, the same paper, in an editorial on a sermon preached by Bishop Tuttle, of the Episcopal Church, in Philadelphia, said : " So far as the institutions of modern Christendom are concerned, we candidly confess our lack of confidence in their power to do anything for us. . . . We have got so far beyond them through the revelations of the Almighty vouchsafed in these latter days, that we look back upon their teachings as a man reverts to the alphabet of his school-days, and we remember their powerless forms and spiritless ceremonies as mere playthings compared with the higher things of the kingdom to which the system they call *Mormonism* has introduced us."

Thus we see that Christianity is discounted by the Mormons from the very start ; and can we, then, hope to accomplish its overthrow by the ordinary means? From its peculiar relations to Christianity, must we not in reason and fairness regard the Mormon Church, as we must the Roman Catholic Church and even Mohammedanism, as being not utterly false, so much as a mingling of error with truth? It is, therefore, a perversion of Christianity. There is genuine Gospel enough in the Mormon creed to save it from the grave. We are, therefore, to look for a repudiation of the false rather than the destruction of both false and true together.

And what would be better calculated to effect this end than the colonization and educational scheme, which we have already advocated as the surest and easiest means to overcome the political and social evils of the system?

The Roman Catholic system is in many respects similar to the Mormon system; and see what intelligence and a surrounding atmosphere of pure Christian truth has done for Roman Catholicism in our land! What a vast difference there is between the system here and the same system in Mexico, Brazil, Spain, or Italy! There is a difference almost as wide as the hemispheres. Take a Roman Catholic from our land to Brazil or Spain, and he will scarcely recognize his religion in that religion called there by the same name. And what has brought about this difference? The American Roman Catholic has been surrounded by intelligence and a free, pure, Christian society. These two things have so operated upon American Roman Catholicism as to greatly reform it and almost radically change it, while they did not antagonize it in a spirit of rancor. How wonderful the revolution! And it has not ceased yet, but is ever going on. The same things would thus be done, we believe, for Mormonism.

1. *A larger intelligence* would surely modify or wholly set aside the claims of the priesthood to the possession of divine authority and power, and would relegate to the realm of oblivion such outlandish doctrines as *baptisms for the dead.* As Froude says, "Ignorance is the dominion of absurdity."

And, from the same cause, the demand would gradually spring up for pulpit teaching, couched in a far better spirit, and of much higher intellectual character. The presence of a few intelligent Gentiles has already put to shame and almost banished from religious assemblies those harangues which in days not very remote were accustomed to combine in about equal measure the profane, the obscene, and the brutal.

2. And, then, *the introduction of Gentile colonists* in

large numbers would naturally increase the force of effective preaching missionaries, and they would then be supported, not by the churches in other parts of our land, but by the Utah colonists themselves. In this way we would have *more missionaries at less expense*, and they would accomplish more in the end than an aggressive force, such as we now have, though it were increased tenfold.

Then the Territory would be fairly flooded with Gospel institutions of every sort. In every Mormon town there would be a school and a church; and there being in every community a few who in character and life would be truly Christlike, they, aided by the sharp criticisms of a free press, would cuttingly and most effectually rebuke the seriously lax morals of the Mormon Church; and before long it would be found to be politic and necessary in sheer self-defence to remove from Church leadership whoever in walk and conversation would fail to conform to what is at least decent.

It is most likely that in this way the better elements in Mormondom would be led, unconsciously perhaps, to assert their force, and work out through grace a religious reformation. The leaven of revolt is slowly working now. It is well known that many Mormons do not countenance polygamy, and the time may yet come when this view shall prevail, notwithstanding the alleged revelations in the case. And there may come a time when, with polygamy, other false doctrines will be questioned or rejected. And thus reformed, purified, and made fit to live, we may expect to see Mormonism continue for generations a sect fairly Christian, although it would doubtless have many peculiar points; or there may come, through the workings of the Gospel in this subtle way, such a division in belief among the Mormon ranks as to rend asunder the entire Mormon organism.

To this work of internal reformation let us direct our forces. Let the Christians of our land arise in all their might and endeavor to have schools planted all over the Territory of Utah, that intelligence and freedom may be widely disseminated; and let them form Colonization Aid Societies to induce Christian families to emigrate to Utah, and settle in every Mormon town and hamlet. Through *the faithful representation and living of the Gospel* I have all hope.

In strict accord with this belief, Rev. Arthur T. Pierson, D.D., pastor of the Bethany Church, Philadelphia, in the *Homiletic Review*, October, 1885, said: "Salt Lake Valley needs nothing more to-day than colonies of Christian tradesmen. Mormonism should be confronted with the witness of a Christian community, consecrated workmen in all the learned professions and departments of industry; Christian families free from the taint of polygamy and full of the rich blessing of the normal household." Likewise, Judge Osborne, of Utah, wrote recently as follows: "An excellent way to do good with little or no cost would be the location of Christian families in the Mormon towns. . . . The Mormon priesthood insist upon the complete isolation of their dupes from Christian civilization. They say, 'You must live your religion;' they obey, and the result is bitter fruit. Let a few Christian families ' live *their* religion' in their presence, and the darkness of prejudice and superstition would roll away like the mist before the morning sun."

Yes, put in every Mormon town a few noble Christian families, consecrated men and women, who in character and life shall exhibit the sweet spirit of the Man of Nazareth, who by example and precept shall show a more excellent way, and presently error will depart, and iniquity hide its head abashed. Let the various denominations combine and co-öperate against the common foe in that silent yet most effective way, and the Mormon Puzzle will be solved, and solved forever. Let us all labor to this end.

> " O Christ, our land for thee ;
> Naught less we crave,
> That Thou supreme mayst be
> From wave to wave.
> Naught less we ask of Thee,
> Our prayer unceasingly,
> Our land for Thee,
> All, all for Thee."

THE END.

www.ingramcontent.com/pod-product-compliance
Lightning Source LLC
Chambersburg PA
CBHW020842160426
43192CB00007B/754